Place Settings in Time

One Woman's Legacy

Barbara McCranie

Copyright © 2008 Lisa Haneberg

All rights reserved. The book, or parts thereof, may not be reproduced in any form without permission from the publisher; exceptions are made for brief excerpts used in public reviews.

ISBN: 978-0-6151-8689-4

Table of Contents

INTRODUCTION	7
CHAPTER 1 – THE CHINA CABINET	8
CHAPTER 2 - GREAT-AUNT MARGARET: DIGNITARY OF PROPRIETY	16
CHAPTER 3 - LOLA: THE FIRST LADY OF DELL FARM	20
CHAPTER 4 - BETTY: THE TALL ONE	34
CHAPTER 5 - THE ENGLISHWOMAN UPSETS THE TEA CART	44
CHAPTER 6 - OUR FIRST DINING ROOM: THE FIRST MCDONALDS	49
CHAPTER 7 - MY HOME: MY TABLE	60
CHAPTER 8 - MONICA SETS HER TABLE	69
CHAPTER 9 - A NEW ROLE: A NEW TABLE	77
CHAPTER 10 - FULL CIRCLE: A CHINA CABINET IN MY KITCHEN	83
AFTERWORD	86

In loving memory of

Barbara McCranie

October 14, 1932 – April 13, 2006

The records left by the ceramic art have furnished keys to many a secret, which would otherwise remain locked. They reflect manners, customs, tastes of the times to which they belong and by their help we may not only therefore study the present but if we choose enter a wide gateway to the past....

Lippincott's Magazine, 1876

Introduction

Since the beginning of time women have gathered their families around the table to nourish their bodies and feed their souls. They laid their table to serve and honor those gathered. Our ancestors moved their china across oceans in the holds of cargo ships and across the prairies in covered wagons to allow a semblance of graceful living in a crude New World. From the humble log cabin to the White House, food presentation was part of the art of socialization.

With the passing of time and wars, new products, communications, transportation, and education evolved. Women were able to pursue careers while managing their homes and families. As women's roles changed, fine china began to lose its habitat: punctual diners in their best attire, table linens, silver, crystal, and dining rooms all fell victim to a more casual lifestyle. With food preparation faster and easier, its presentation was often dictated by whimsy.

Place Settings in Time: One Woman's Legacy follows my journey from my rural homestead, where the large kitchen was the center of my universe, to the present day, where the world is my playground. En route, I set my table in a barnyard and onboard a boat floating at the foot of the Stature of Liberty.

We have a need to explore our traditions and decide how to feature them in our contemporary lifestyles. This is how we celebrate our being.

Chapter 1 – The China Cabinet

At the White House:

It all began with Martha Washington. When she took up residence in the President's house in New York City, the tableware was China export porcelain in common use in Colonial America.

By 1904 a china collection was displayed in the ground floor corridor of the White House. The north wall cabinet showed the new Theodore Roosevelt service (top shelf). The Benjamin Harrison service (second shelf). Various pieces gained during the Cleveland and McKinley administrations (third shelf). And the Grant and Lincoln buff-band services (bottom shelf).

At the Dell Farm:

It all began with our ancestors. They moved their china across oceans in the holds of ships and across the prairies in covered wagons, so they could set a proper table in the New World. By 1932, a china cabinet at the Dell Farm displayed a collection of heirlooms.

The woman buried the crystal knife rests in a bag of flour, then stowed the bundle in the bow of the canoe. She had transported them safely across the turbulent Atlantic—now she must get them upriver to her new home. The sparkling rests were family trophies — stock for a proper table. She shivered realizing she could be called on to sacrifice them, barter them, or dump them in the river: anything to assure the safe transport of the children, ax, and flour.

It was 1823 when this family from Scotland landed in the New World. They loaded their two small children and bundles of essential supplies into a canoe and paddled up a long river, looking for a place to settle. They came ashore at a sandy bay, and with their ax, blazed a trail five miles north to a fertile dell covered in giant timber. My ancestors had landed where Grandpa Charlie would one day build a summer cottage. They had claimed land where my first home would stand. The woman had smuggled crystal for the china cabinet.

I am Barbara. I was born in 1932, twenty minutes after my sister Betty. We arrived at Dell Farm where we grew up side-by-side, each with a unique view of our being. We shared a rich family legacy—a legacy showcased in the china cabinet and shrouded in mystery by an old letter hidden there.

Dell Farm had 200 acres of cleared land and the house was a large two-story, six-bedroom structure. The kitchen was the hub of my childhood existence. This is where Mother baked cookies, braided my hair, and simmered pots of soup on the back of the wood stove. My clothes were made in the kitchen. I played, did my homework, and had my Saturday night bath there. And three times each day I sat down to a set table with my family.

A big round wood table sat in the center, but like a silver slipper in a cow pasture, the china cabinet dominated the room. It displayed my family's credentials—our heritage. I remember what was on each shelf, in each drawer, and behind each door. The top shelf held a bevy of fine china cups and saucers, each a different shape, pattern, and origin. They looked like flowers in an English garden at springtime. If company arrived in time for afternoon tea, we used the cups from the china cabinet. Other small pieces of china were on the top shelf, too—a candy dish, butter dishes, cake plates, and a gravy boat—made by Spode, Carnival Glass, and Wedgewood.

The second shelf displayed memorabilia. A cracked and glued blue and white ABC plate was there. When my father told the story about learning his alphabet from the old plate, he talked about his mother and his grandmother. I pictured him sitting in school holding the plate—perhaps dropping it—as he turned it to read the letters. A burgundy cordial glass with "Lola" etched on its flange was a gift to my mother from her home economics teacher. Proper manners and table setting had been important subjects at Mother's school. A silver baby spoon with "Iverson" engraved on its bowl held a prominent spot on the shelf—like the spot my brother held in the family as the eldest and only male heir. My favorite item on the shelf was a dainty china tea set that belonged to our older sister, Laura's, dolls—a gift from a grandmother I never knew. A grandmother who, it was whispered, smoked a pipe.

The third shelf showcased cut glass. There was a set of diamond-cut crystal knife rests (like two small dumbbells) used to hold greasy knives off the tablecloth. Some believed that an uncle in Scotland cut his teeth on them. A tall cut-glass water pitcher with a tarnished silver spout served as a vase for fresh flowers. The biggest and heaviest piece was a three-legged fruit bowl the size of a large pumpkin. When the sun hit the third shelf, it sent pieces of rainbows dancing across the kitchen.

An old letter with a pressed flower folded in its pages was moved from shelf to shelf. Mother sometimes moved the letter when she replaced pieces used to set the table, and sometimes after long periods of contemplation. When she moved the letter her face was set and determined: it was not a happy face.

In the cabinet drawer, ivory-handled knives and forks wrapped in blue flannel rolls—a gift sent to my mother from my father while he served overseas during the First World War. Stacked behind the two bottom doors was a drab brown and white English china service for twelve, by Johnson Brothers, a wedding gift to my mother and father.

The china cabinet was in the kitchen because we didn't have a dining room. The enormous kitchen held two couches—for naps or a place to read or be close to the stove and the soup if you were ill. The front wall was the work center—first the kitchen cabinet filled with everyday dishes and utensils, then the wood burning stove, the cold storage, and a dumbwaiter. We used a hand pump at the sink in one corner. In the opposite corner the china cabinet stood tall and proud. Stairs up to the bedrooms and down to the basement were on the back wall.

A big round maple table with a scar the shape of a flatiron sat in the middle of the room. The table was set for three meals each day, and in between it served as a desk for homework and letter writing, and a table for board games. Every Tuesday morning Mother did the ironing on the table.

My first memories around the big table include my twin sister Betty and our Bunnykins dishes. We each had a plate, a cereal bowl, and a cup, painted with furry brown bunnies running around the rims and bunny families doing family things in the center. The bunnies played hide-and-seek with my food and helped me get rid of my porridge. Our place settings were by Royal Doulton. I knew they were special and we used them every day.

> *From Betty: I still have a Bunnykins plate in my china cabinet. Not sure if it's yours or mine.*

The first floor contained two other rooms - a parlor and a guest bedroom. They were usually closed and thus cold in the winter. The parlor was used for formal gatherings. Adults sat stiff and straight and talked about the state of affairs. When the minister visited, he read his Bible and prayed in the parlor. We took piano lessons there—Mother had illusions about the twins performing duets. The best parlor time was on Sunday when Mother played the piano. She would fling her hands up into the air and bang them back down on the keys as she played *Onward Christian Soldiers*, and Betty and I would march up and down the room, keeping time to the music.

The guest bedroom was nicely furnished. It had a washstand with a porcelain washbasin and water pitcher. The chamber pot under the bed matched the set.

Betty remarks: I always thought of the guest bedroom as Aunt Margaret's room. The only other person to sleep there was Miss Argue. Do you remember her, Barbara? An elderly teacher, tall, with gray hair and sometimes a corset stay popping through her sweater. She roomed and boarded at the Palmers' near the school. One Sunday she called and asked Mom if she could come for supper, sleep over, and walk to school with us in the morning. The guestroom was quickly heated for the unexpected guest. Other sleepovers used whatever upstairs space was available.

> *Betty, I don't remember Miss Argue well, but I do remember the sweater—pink with an open stitch, matted and shrunk—and I remember the corset stay.*

The upstairs had five bedrooms, each with a china chamber pot under the bed. Washing and bathing were done downstairs in the kitchen. Later a bathroom was installed in the smallest bedroom, and the chamber pots became objets d'art. The new bathroom was the first place I could lock the door and isolate myself. I would sit on the toilet and think about private things or stand in front of the big mirror and examine my body.

> *Betty adds: The upstairs back hall was our inside play area. We had our table and chairs; our dolls were tucked into their respective beds. I remember the new store-bought blue crib, a homemade double bed, and Laura's little cradle. The table was set with miniature fiesta-style dishes.*

We had identical dolls, but we knew which one belonged to whom, and we never considered switching babies to make sets of twins. I set and reset the table; I served mostly cereal and cookies. Today I use the store-bought crib for a magazine rack.

There was a dell (a hollow) behind the house—our private ski slopes. And a wooded gully where we played in the creek.

> *Betty's bit: Thimbleberry Hill separated the gully from the dell. The hill yielded at least a cup of tiny perfect berries in the early summer. Legend had it and Laura, our older and wiser sister, said that it was once a family burying ground. Legend could have been confusing berrying with burying.*

Dad rotated six fenced fields between crops and pasture. A cluster of outbuildings stood behind the house—a cow barn, feed and equipment compound, tool shed, and chicken coop. The women were in charge of the chicken coop. I hated gathering eggs and I usually ended up with both chicken poop and hen pecks on my hands.

We cut the grass in front of the house with a rotary push mower. We often spread a blanket under the big maple tree and shelled peas or played with our dolls. The vegetable garden was between the lawn and the road.

Our outside playhouse was nestled at the side of the house. Wild cucumber vines covered the chicken wire walls and it was the perfect setting for tea parties and telling secrets. We dressed our dolls and served them tea at a little table. We tried to dress the cat. Rex, the dog, would sometimes cooperate and sit pretty with a colorful bandanna around his neck. Visiting aunts sat on a long bench and sipped colored water from our tiny cups while pointing their little finger toward the sky. Our cousins were the most cooperative afternoon tea guests.

> *Betty interrupts: Barbara, I remember one summer you thought we should spruce up the place. We agreed the floor should be the priority. A neighbor kid told us he used pop and beer bottle tops, collected from his family store, tapping them into a dirt floor, creating a wonderful mosaic. We were suitably impressed, but because we had no bottle tops at our house, you instead salvaged the center of a discarded braided rag rug to cozy up the place.*

We communicated with family and friends by telephone and letters. Magazines, newspapers, the catalogue, and a radio connected us with the outside world. The telephone—larger than a breadbox—hung on the kitchen wall. A cluster of farms shared a party line. Each household had an exclusive number of long and short rings. Our number was two long rings. To contact someone on the line, we picked up the receiver, listened to make sure the line was free, and then used the crank to make the sequence of rings. To contact someone on another party line, we rang the operator and she connected the two lines. Most conversations happened on our party line. We knew who was calling by their unique long and short ring. The operator's ring was mechanical and distinct. We could listen in on conversations and often did. This is how we found out when Mrs. Bean was expecting another baby and when one of the Stark children fell off the roof. The telephone was the fire alarm—one continual long ring—and the neighbors responded with their pails and shovels. I remember a couple of fire calls. The few long-distance calls usually carried bad news. Long-distance social communications were by letter.

> *Betty's comments: Telephone conversations were brief and to the point. If the party line was occupied and the line was urgently needed, it was quite acceptable to interrupt and ask for the line. Our family did a bit of telemarketing—Mom unloaded overabundant crops of strawberries or raspberries*

(which her darling daughters had picked) and Dad found buyers for grain.

We wrote letters to distant family at the kitchen table using a fountain pen. Much thought and care went into their composition and into our penmanship. While our facial expressions reflected the nature of the content, the details of our letters were never discussed. Like the letter in the china cabinet, letters were respected and their contents held confidential. With dramatic flair we folded, addressed, and stamped each letter. We carried our letters with care and reverence to the mailbox at the road.

The mailman left the weekly newspaper and Mother's monthly *Good Housekeeping*. We learned about the world around us through magazine articles and advertisements. The most anticipated piece of mail was the catalogue. It was our marketplace. Everyone scurried for his or her first preview, and everyone had a wish list: a sloop sleigh, hair ribbons, a doll. A new catalogue was the topic of conversations for weeks.

We turned the radio on at noon for the news and *The Farm Broadcast*. We sat quietly while the men listened to the crop and weather forecasts. By midafternoon, Mother tuned in *Ma Perkins*, and everyone gathered around in the evening for the antics of Jack Benny, Fibber McGee and Molly. For adventure we listened with rapt attention to *Superman* and *The Shadow*.

A whistle stop train was our only mass transport. Its passengers were mostly cattle. We had a family car and made weekly trips to town for supplies—usually on Saturday night. Two or three times a year, we made long trips, of 20 to 120 miles, to visit relatives. Betty and I had a horse for transportation to and from school. The tractor and farm truck were the most important vehicles. They stayed on the farm property and created revenue.

Betty chimes in: We did have a car but the roads were not plowed, and for many months we had to rely on horse-drawn conveyances. Dad would make a weekly trip to town for supplies. Sometimes a sleigh-pool was arranged with neighbors. For church, the chariot of choice was a horse-drawn cutter. And, yes, we had a horse. One autumn day Dad returned from a sale with Beauty in tow. She was a retired racehorse — black and beautiful. She was a substitute for the bicycles we had begged for and never received. Why? Because she was all-weather transportation. That horse was responsible for one of my seven critical life choices.

My childhood was spent on the Dell Farm. Betty was my constant companion—part of my being. Our life revolved around setting down to the table three times each day. I will now introduce you to the women who set our table—Great-Aunt Margaret and, my mother, Lola.

Our world was small.

China our heritage.

The catalogue our marketplace.

Chapter 2 - Great-Aunt Margaret: Dignitary of Propriety

At the White House:

Eleanor Roosevelt, America's most distinguished First Lady, used her position to create a bridge between the presidency and the people. From 1945 to 1950 she was a delegate to the U.N. Assembly, Chairperson of UNESCO's Commission on Human Rights, and America's roving ambassador of goodwill. When Eleanor Roosevelt commenced her duties as First Lady, the Lenox china originally ordered during the Wilson presidency (1918) was in use.

At the Same Time:

Great-Aunt Margaret visited her nieces and nephews as a dignitary of propriety.

Great-Aunt Margaret had delicate skin, a weak stomach, thinning hair, a morning dress, an afternoon dress, a social dress, a tailored suit, and a magnificent set of Theodore Haviland china. She lived in an uptown apartment in the city. You could sit on her second-floor balcony and hear streetcars rattling along their tracks on the way to department stores, movie theaters, and soda fountains. Great Auntie filled the time slot vacated by my grandmothers. She was a widow and childless so she had missed out on cultivated maternal traits. But her nieces and nephews were her family and, more like a diplomatic dignitary than an aunt, she made annual visits to their rural homes. She oversaw the arrangements for all social events and decorating projects. Propriety was her specialty.

When Great-Aunt Margaret arrived in her tailored suit, her suitcase (she called it her valise) was immediately taken to the guest bedroom and the china water pitcher filled with tepid water. The door to the bedroom did not close tightly, so Betty and I could peek through the crack at the hinge and watch Auntie's personal pampering. Her morning toilet never varied. She poured water into the hand-painted china basin and dipped a cheesecloth sack filled with rolled oats into the water—soap for her delicate skin. With a soft facecloth she washed her face—then all folding body parts. Next the pink velvet powder puff gave off a generous dusting of talcum powder.

It was an amazing spectacle when she laced her corset. From the laying out and positioning of undergarments to the grand finale, it was a precisely choreographed event. Lying on her back she laced, hooked, pushed, and pulled the two layers of boned armor until her innards were compacted. Then she put on her morning dress and sat down at the vanity to arrange her hair. She heated curling tongs in the chimney of a coal oil lamp. She wrapped a small section of long thin hair around the tongs, held and released it until her hair was a thick-looking mass of wavy ringlets. Then she gathered the hair, twisted it into a bun, and secured it at the nape of her neck with two tortoiseshell hairpins. A splash of toilet water and Great-Aunt Margaret made her entrance to the kitchen for breakfast.

Like the Queen of England she dominated the big table. Her diet contained no fat, no spice, and only puréed meat. But the delivery made every morsel a succulent appetizer. A cup of hot water with "just a drop of milk" served in a china cup as delicate as her skin. A coddled egg[1] in an eggcup sat on a pink glass plate. A Wedgwood bowl held cream-of-wheat—with a pinch of brown sugar dead center. A slice of dry toast cut in triangles was arranged on a doily and set on a china plate. Half a canned peach reflected through a crystal nappy. Like Auntie herself, it was all in the presentation.

She was not a doer. She was a consultant and her stay was abuzz with plans. How to adjust hems to the season's length. Where to place a tieback on the curtain so it looked best from both the road and the room. A suitable centerpiece for a cousin's bridal shower – a chamber pot full of lilacs. The right color hose for a person in mourning.

Bridal showers, church socials, christenings, and weddings were all scheduled around Great Auntie's visit. And before she arrived

---

[1] Coddled Egg: An egg cooked in its shell – placed in cold water, brought just below a boil, then set off the heat for three minutes before serving.

we made sure to inspect the china, polish the silver, and shine the crystal. As Mother inventoried and cleaned our china cabinet, she lifted the old letter and Aunt Margaret remarked, "You still have that letter?" Mother said, "Yes, it's still an issue."

Auntie wore her morning dress when planning, her afternoon dress to visit sites, and her social dress tastefully accessorized to camouflage its frequent appearances. Her accessories included a long string of pearls and a natural linen hankie with tatted[2] edging secured at her hipline with a cameo pin. A cascade of silk forget-me-nots graced her left shoulder, and she had white lace gloves to wear or hold.

Betty adds: When there was a chill in the air, a little fox scarf accompanied the pinstriped suit. It had paws and a tail! The head had beady little eyes. A clasp opened and closed the jaws that snapped onto one of the appendages, holding the little critter in place.

Auntie sipped a lot of hot water—always from the best china cup in the house. She stood tall and worked the room while the other ladies sat on the chairs lining the walls.

Betty reminisces: Barbara, remember the summer we each got to spend a week at Aunt M's? I loved being separated from home and you, and having Auntie's undivided attention in such posh surroundings. I spent a lot of time in her bathroom scrubbing my elbows and knees. Tanned limbs were foreign to her. She thought I was dirty.

Yes, Betty, I remember. Mother was making us new dresses for our trip to the city. Of course, you went first in your new dress. It was harvest time and Mother was too busy to finish my dress, so she quickly shortened yours for my trip.

---

[2] Tatting: Delicate homemade lace formed by looping and knotting with a single cotton thread and a small shuttle.

Auntie kept abreast of fashion trends for sophisticated women with her monthly subscription to *Harper's Bazaar*. She read the daily newspaper and scanned the advertisements for news and current trends. Her city apartment had electric appliances, and she received two or three stations on her console radio. It was part of her daily routine to sit at her desk in the dining room to write letters and make phone calls. The quality of her writing paper and the nib on her pen met exacting specifications. Her ink was a strange green color. I knew she didn't write the letter in our china cabinet. Letters were sent and mail received in one of a bank of mailboxes in the vestibule of the building. A cradle telephone sat on the desk with a phone directory and address book. If she made a long-distance call she logged it with the date and the starting and ending times.

For travel outside the city, Great-Aunt Margaret took the train if connections were satisfactory. Most of the time one of her nieces or nephews would tote her in their automobile. In the city limits a taxicab was available and arranged for well in advance if the occasion merited such extravagance, but she used the streetcar at will.

Some of my most magical childhood moments were at Auntie's apartment in the city. Streetcar rides to department stores (with elevators). I saw my first movie (*Stage Door Canteen*) there and I watched the Ice Escapades at the coliseum and sipped an ice cream soda at Woolworth's. I enjoyed walking to the park along tree-lined sidewalks and sitting on the balcony listening to the sounds of the city. I remember squeezing the air out of the upright vacuum cleaner and wrapping the garbage in newspaper, tying it with string like a gift, and dropping it down the garbage chute. I ate in her dining room – with more pieces of fine china than I knew what to do with. And, I was the princess in this fairytale as I sipped hot chocolate from Auntie's charming little cocoa set.

> Visions of Grandeur.
> Through a crack in the door.
> From a streetcar.
> Over a cup of hot chocolate.

Chapter 3 - Lola: The First Lady of Dell Farm

At the White House:

When Anna Eleanor Roosevelt came to the White House in 1933, she understood social conditions better than any of her predecessors had and she transformed the role of First Lady accordingly. When she learned that the china on hand was insufficient to set a large formal dinner, she ordered new china. The Lenox china with the Roosevelt crest was considered the state china from 1935 until 1951.

At the Same Time:

Lola works the house at Dell Farm.

My mother's name was "Lola," and she worked the house. She understood social conditions and the needs of her family, and she patterned her role accordingly. She used her degree in domestic science to fine-tune the system and add a touch of graciousness to our rural existence. She was the First Lady at the Dell Farm.

Her gait, like her demeanor, was regal, determined, and choreographed—yet comfortable. When she hesitated to make a decision, she would wipe her hands on her apron or, if the change dictated, she would turn her apron inside out or reach for a different apron; but, always in stride—always a lady.

Food was Lola's first priority. At the Dell Farm, food preparation started with the planting of seeds and breeding of livestock. A long, painstaking, and never-ending production line filled the basement with row upon row of sealed jars, a full root cellar, and an earthenware jar of sauerkraut. The daily manipulating of the Holstein's teats produced bottles of fresh milk and thick cream, a crock of fresh churned butter, and wheels of cheese. In summer the fruit and vegetables were fresh from the garden. In winter pieces of meat were sawed from frozen quarters hanging in the shed: we ate roasts, roasts, and more roasts. Nothing was allowed to spoil: excesses were canned or preserved for future use.

> *Betty complains: We always had lots to eat, but it did get boring. When the strawberries were in season, we ate strawberries morning, noon, and night. We lusted for the first ripe tomato, the first cob of corn; but after a week, it did get ahead of us. Baskets of overly ripe tomatoes, bushels of corn, and no need to ask, "What's for supper?" We had been picking it, cleaning it, and preserving it all day.*

Lola did some of her best tweaking in the kitchen. She filled bottles with jam, jelly, preserves, pickles, chicken, and beef. She labeled and dated each jar. The vintage classified its quality and it was shelved accordingly; exceptional product went on the top shelf. Some bottles were treasured for years before they found a worthy table.

Lola filled tin boxes with freshly baked biscuits, muffins, bread, cookies, and pie, leaving her personal brand on each piece. Her handiwork could be identified by the fluting around her pies, slits in the top crust, beads of sugar shining on the meringue, her sugar cookies by their pinked edge and one plump seedless raisin in the center, the sliver of maraschino cherry crowning the top of each macaroon, the milk and brown sugar topping on her tea biscuits, squares cut square with a very sharp knife, cinnamon rolls that were cut then rolled, not rolled then cut, and a dab of her chokecherry jelly on rice or blanc mange pudding. Each morsel was cherished and served after careful consideration. What would life be without dessert? Most of our food was produced and prepared on the farm, but there was always a store list.

> *Betty elaborates: Mom usually phoned in her grocery order. There was seldom time for her to make a trip to town during the week. Her order would be boxed and ready when Dad or a neighbor was in town on farm business. Flour, sugar, tea, coffee, dried fruit, rolled oats, and vinegar were basic needs purchased in large quantities. The grocery store carried some dry goods, and occasionally shoes or boots arrived with the groceries. Mom would have traced a foot on cardboard and*

sent it to town with whoever was picking up supplies. The shopkeeper would send a few pair to choose from and the rest would be returned on the next trip to town.

The laying of the table created the appropriate presentation for this meticulous production, and Lola set the table with care three times a day, 365 days each year. The table showcased Lola's upbringing and education. Cutlery was often mismatched, but always lined up with each piece in its proper place. She placed large plates and side plates to cradle the food being served. Glasses and cups were ready for cold and hot beverages. There were serving dishes for each presentation: platters for meat, bowls for vegetables, a gravy boat for the gravy, relish dishes for pickles from the cellar or fresh radish from the garden, and cheese—always cheese. A silver tray with thick slices of fresh baked bread sat next to the butter dish filled with salty, churned butter. Jars and cooking pots were never put on our table.

The laying of the table was the proof of our success: the framing of our credentials. Lola's table was highly regarded among the neighbors and townspeople. Salesmen, dairy inspectors, and the mailman all set their sights on the Dell Farm at mealtime. It was common practice to set another plate at the last minute, and there was fierce competition among the farm wives when it came to laying the table for the harvest crew.

The Rawleigh salesman rattled up to the kitchen door yearly. His black sedan was loaded to the roof with salves, ointments, spices, and flavorings. Lola had her shopping list ready, but she wiped her hands, put on a clean apron, and walked out to the traveling store to enjoy the spiel and inhale the vapors. She inquired about the salesman's family and invariably ended up asking him to stay for a bite to eat.

The dairy inspector's bi-annual visits were scheduled, and he arrived in time for the evening milking. He drove right to the barn where the cows were lined up in their stanchions, their udders bulging. The inspector worked in a suit and tie wearing white gloves as he took milk samples from each cow. He used chemicals to test the milk and recorded his findings in a worn ledger. His presence was respected despite his foreign persona, and when the milking was finished he was asked to stay for supper. He would accept saying, "I remember what a fine table the Missus sets." By the time the supper table was cleared and the lamps lit, he had wangled an invitation to spend the night—guaranteeing breakfast in the morning.

> *Betty, on breakfast: Every morning, rolled oats or cream of wheat was ladled into our Bunnykins bowls from a little aluminum porridge pot. Jam topped thick slices of toast or, if Dad had been compensated for his services to the local beekeeper or sugar bush operator, we enjoyed honey or maple syrup. I remember a different offering when the men folk sat down for breakfast. They had been doing chores for a couple of hours; they were ravenous. Fried potatoes, warmed-over baked beans, eggs, a thick slice of cheese—lots of whatever was available.*

For a long time our grandfather delivered the mail. He just walked into the kitchen, hung his fedora on a hook, pulled up a chair, and waited for dinner to be served. He had other children on his route, but he fancied our table and Lola's pie.

Pie, pie, and more pie—we had a virtual assembly line as we rolled pastry, sliced fruit, spiced pumpkin, squeezed lemon, flavored custard, and peaked meringue. The threshing gang was coming— let the competition begin. We set the table with the same diligence that family and guest meals received, except the meat was not carved at the table and the women did not sit down with the men. It was a banquet for country squires in overalls. A long table was set up outside the kitchen door with basins and pitchers of water, and each man washed and removed his hat before entering for dinner. The big table was extended with all its leaves, and the threshers sat elbow to elbow around its perimeter. Dad sat at one end and encouraged all to dig in. For a while, all attention focused on filling plates. The women kept busy refilling the serving dishes. Lola inspected each dish before we took it to the table: wiping rims, arranging slices, and adding garnish. Then the storytelling began, and between "please pass the ___," there was knee-slapping and laughing as each farmer tried to out tell the other.

When the women removed the dinner plates, it was time for pie. Lola received compliments and smiled as she refilled plates with yet another slice. When the men finally pushed their chairs back from the table, she ran her fingers through her thick auburn hair, turned her apron inside out, and stood at the door to see them back to work. Lola enjoyed being the tall, trim lady of the manor—the attractive farmer's wife.

By-products from the feeding process played an important role in the clothing and laundry detail. Women saved sugar and flour bags to make garments, aprons, curtains, dishtowels, and pillow cases. Fat rendered from pork and beef became the binding ingredient for lye soap. The early flour and sugar bags had to be bleached to remove the product logos, but it didn't take long for the manufacturers to entice the lady's loyalty by sticking easily removed paper advertising over their cotton bags and making some patterned bags in decorator colors. I remember how excited we were when we saw the first sugar bag in color and checks. Sugar bags were finer and smaller than flour bags, and each bag was ear-marked for a much loftier purpose—but the new colored bags were coveted, pilfered, and bartered. Lola created most of her aprons from bags—the apron often more fashionable than the dress it covered. She didn't share her apron patterns, and she was very selective in the choice of bags for their construction.

Many of our pillowcases were bags with embroidered designs and crochet lace edgings. Most tea towels were bags—some were embellished. Tablecloths and napkins made from bags were embroidered, appliquéd, and finished to size with a crochet edge. Betty and I had the greatest bibbed overalls made from bleached flour bags. They had big red buttons, and the buttonholes were worked in red floss. I sometimes wonder if Tommy Hilfiger stole Lola's design.

All these items were Mother's handiwork. She would sew into the late afternoon when the light was good, and even longer if she had enough leftovers to make supper preparation easy.

In the spring there were new garments to be made. Yard goods bought at the general store were cut from patterns ordered from the weekly paper or traced from another garment. She basted these pieces together, fitting them to fall gently over the body, and then sewed them on our treadle machine—a Singer. The hem was most important. It was pinned to the season's length—according to specifications defined by Great-Aunt Margaret.

Winter evenings found Lola relaxing in her favorite chair, knitting sweaters, socks, mittens, gloves, and scarves by lamplight. She produced items made for Betty and me in duplicate—one a little longer than the other. Most times Mother managed to finish both items at the same time. It was like Christmas to get up one morning and find a new outfit pressed and ready to wear. She bought dress suits, stockings, handkerchiefs, underwear, most outer garments, and men's work clothes from the general store or the catalogue.

Betty adds: The big-ticket item in the underwear category was a new corset for Mom. Her brown church dress might have to do for another year, but a new corset was a must. Corsets were available from the catalogue, but our mother's would be made by the regionally acclaimed corsetiere, Mrs. Elliott. Dad would fuss when consulted about the transportation arrangements and appointment time, but all that would be sorted out and Mom would come home with a tissue wrapped, flesh-colored, foundation garment.

My first memory of laundry day included lye soap. Lola kept a big metal can beside the stove, and all fat was rendered and poured into the can—it was a yucky mess. When the can was full, it was time to make soap. The fat was melted, strained, and blended with a can of Gillett's Lye. This caustic mixture was poured into a big pitted metal pan, and when the fatty mixture hardened, it was cut into 4- x 6-inch bars and stored for use.

Monday morning the kitchen became a cluttered obstacle path. The gasoline-powered washing machine was pulled to the middle of the kitchen and encircled by piles of sorted dirty clothes. Big washtubs half full of water had been heating on the wood-burning stove since before dawn. Lola shaved curls of lye soap into a pot of water, and added the slimy liquid to the water in the washing machine. Then, starting with the whites, each pile of clothes was washed, rinsed (some dipped in starch), and pinned to the big umbrella clothesline outside the kitchen door. When the men's dark work clothes were put through the soapy wash and the clear rinse, the water was neither soapy nor clear. By the time the laundry was done and the machine wiped down, it was time to set the dinner table.

After dinner we helped Mother remove the clothes from the lines and put them in big baskets. In the winter the clothes were frozen. Mother once stood the men's long johns in a snowdrift and let Betty and I laugh at the headless ghosts trudging through the snow. Frozen clothes were hung again on inside lines. Finally she folded the dry clothes or, dampened and rolled, packed them ready for ironing the next day. She ironed everything except underwear, hand towels, and the men's overalls.

Tuesday was ironing day. After we cleared the dinner table, Lola took two of the freshly laundered bed sheets and smoothed them over the table. This served two purposes, a pad to iron the clothes on and two ironed sheets. The fire in the range had been carefully tended to a thick bed of red-hot coals. She placed four flatirons on the hot spot and their shared handle was clipped to the iron being used. Lola licked a finger and touched the iron to make sure the temperature was right for each fabric, and from time to time slid the iron over a pad of wax paper to improve its slip. She piled up stacks of ironed pillowcases, tablecloths, napkins, tea towels, aprons, and handkerchiefs. She hung up shirts, dresses, and pants. The kitchen smelled of starch, soap, and steam—clean. Lola proudly put everything away in drawers and closets.

When the laundry was done, Lola indulged herself. She sat down and tuned in Ma Perkins on the radio while she sewed on buttons, turned a collar, or darned socks.

Lola's social outlet was a church group. The Ladies met in the church hall and made garments and quilts for those in need. I remember items for our soldiers during the Second World War. The ladies knit boxes and boxes of yarn into socks and mitts. Mrs. Stark walked around all day with a ball of yarn hanging from her arm—knitting and socializing on the move. Other ladies sat around a quilting frame while others folded bandages. They shared the news they were privy to: the scanty cut on the new underpanties, the availability of sanitary protection, a new pattern, the price of sugar, and a new dress or hat were popular topics. At the end of the afternoon, it was time for tea.

The church hall's kitchen was stocked with a large set of china and a big fancy tin of tea. One of the ladies would put a large kettle of water on a coal oil burner and bring it to a full rolling boil. While the tea was steeping, each lady displayed her cake, cookies, or squares on a china plate. A table was spread with a linen cloth and napkins, and tea was served. It was a special time; a competition, an exhibition, a sharing of accomplishments—validation. The ladies kept up-to-date on local gossip, and our soldiers had warm socks and mitts.

> *Betty comments: I doubt the ladies discussed intimate family conflicts or problems. I'm sure Mother didn't vent the frustration she experienced the day I saw her throw the food ration coupon books at Dad as he banged the door shut and left for town. But she might have told them about the time the hired girl borrowed the hired man's armbands and used them for garters—then returned them to his room stretched and totally useless.*

Lola made frequent telephone calls to check on neighbors and to her father and sisters who lived in the area. We avoided gossiping on the telephone; you never knew who might be listening. She wrote letters to distant relatives, and like the letter in the china cabinet these bore an invisible stamp of confidentiality.

When the roads were open, Saturday night was family night and everyone went to town for supplies and edification. The first priority was finding a good parking spot on Main Street. Then we split up to visit the shops. Mother or Dad gave Betty and I each a nickel, but we could only spend it on ice cream at Uncle Andrew's ice cream parlor. Dad left to lean on the rail in front of the bank with the men who weren't in the bar. Lola visited the general store for groceries and then moved on to the dry goods section. She would look at the set of dishes she fancied and inquire again about the price, then stroll to the yard goods to drape, stretch, and bunch up fabric. Sometimes she would buy a length for a garment. Something was always needed— buttons, thread, yarn, elastic, needles. I remember Lola insisting that a sales clerk special order the right color of tan buttonhole floss so she could finish beige tweed coats for Betty and I in a professional manner.

When we finished walking the street and enjoying our ice cream cones, we returned to sit in the car, where we watched our neighbors scurry between shops with their packages. Some would stop and chat through the open window. Lola often mused to herself as she watched this parade, mumbling things like, *I guess Jean bought that housedress she was looking at; I wonder how she can do that when their taxes aren't paid and another baby is on the way.* Sometimes Dad bought a brick of ice cream before he returned to the car. We then drove the five miles home and immediately sat around the table to share our stories about the evening while enjoying big bowls of melting ice cream. I remember one Saturday night when Dad told us of talk about an electric power line coming through. Lola was so excited she dribbled ice cream down the front of her new blouse. Betty and I talked under the bed covers that night about the possibility of a refrigerator with the freezer full of all different flavors of ice cream.

Sunday was a day of rest, and work was limited to milking the cows and feeding the family and the animals. Everyone put on their Sunday best and went to church. Lola wore a hat and gloves and Dad a fedora. The men took their hats off at the church door and held them on their laps. The women left their hats on and often pulled the veils over their eyes. After the sermon everyone shook hands with Reverend Folks and then mingled with the congregation and talked about the week's happenings.

> *Betty adds: Sunday after church was a big visiting time. I would venture that the main reason our dad went to church was the visiting afterward and occasionally a little nap during the sermon.*

The men did not loosen their ties and the women did not take off their hats. Lola straightened Betty's and my hats, pushed our hair back behind our ears with a dampened finger, and tightened the ribbon under our chin while she cautioned us not to run through the high grass with our good shoes on. She always talked with her sister, and sometimes her family came home with us for dinner. Sunday dinner was usually cold sliced roast, pickles, scalloped potatoes, and lots of dessert. We set the table with the best cloth, and we ate in our Sunday clothes. We would tuck our napkins in at our necks, swing our fancy feet, talk about pleasant things, and make plans for the coming week.

Lola drove the family car, but I know she didn't have a driver's license—perhaps no one did. She drove to her father's house and to the corner store beside the school, but I don't remember her ever driving to town. My older siblings rode their bicycles to high school in town. In the winter, when the roads were blocked, they roomed and boarded in town and came home on weekends. My brother, Iverson, drove the family car on special occasions, and my sister, Laura, helped out driving the tractor. But neither owned a car while they lived on the farm.

When Betty and I started to school, Lola drove us and came back to pick us up at lunchtime (We needed our afternoon nap.). When we started attending full-time, we would walk or ski. We had our horse, Beauty; but Beauty made Betty nervous, and that horse didn't like spending the day in the school's woodshed. She was soon put out to pasture. We liked to ski to school in the winter; at recess and noon we were allowed to slide on the hill behind the school.

Betty comments: Gordon Alexander had a handsome set of homemade red sloop sleighs that were envied by all— and you in particular, Barbara. I know you remember Gordie's sloops. You thought you were the Queen of the Hill when Gordie invited you to ride with him.

Betty and I attended a two-room elementary school at The Corner—a crossroad where there was a little country store with gas pumps, the school, a church and church hall, a cheese factory, and a cemetery. The Corner was one mile from the Dell Farm. The school had a partition most of the way down the middle. On one side were grades one, two, and three, and on the other the big grades—four, five, and six. The teacher's desk sat at the end of the partition at the back and the wood stove stood at the end of the partition in the front. Clothes hooks lined the front wall. We called it a two-room school, but we only had one teacher. This set-up allowed us to pick up advanced training from the lessons taught in the higher grades and review from the lower grades. Sometimes there was no one in a grade, but most classes had two or three students.

Betty expounds: We always looked forward to Friday afternoons. Some sort of entertainment was encouraged to end the week on a high note. We might have a spelling bee, a

> debate, or a geography match. We held Red Cross meetings where the talented, and not so talented, could perform while the rest of us knitted scarves for soldiers. Dalton Elliot was the school idol. He had a guitar. He could play that guitar and he could sing. I still remember the words to "Wabash Cannonball" and "There's a Star-Spangled Banner Waving Somewhere." I think "Wild Colonial Boy" was also in his repertoire.

In the winter we had a hot lunch program; the families took turns bringing a kettle of soup. It was put on the wood stove to simmer until noon when our teacher filled everyone's cup. Days when there wasn't soup, everyone brought a jar of milk, put it on the window sill to keep it cold (or freeze), and before noon all the milk was dumped in a big pot and warmed to make hot chocolate. We ate at our desks.

> Betty laments: I hated soup day. After seeing what appeared to be a portion of a cow's udder floating in one pot of soup, I only ate Mom's. But when it was our turn to bring the pot of soup, we had to endure the cutter ride to school with Maurice Fleury. Remember, he was a hired hand Mom had commissioned to get her prized pot of soup safely to school and placed on the stove. She sent a note saying that she had provided enough soup for generous servings and her soup must not be watered down.

We had field trips from school. We walked next door to the cheese factory where the cheese maker showed us where our milk was dumped and gave us a handful of curds to eat. He had huge furnaces stoked with six-foot slab wood. When they opened the big doors to throw in the long wood, I thought I saw Shadrach, Meshach, and Abednego walking in the flames. That night when I said my prayers, I asked God's forgiveness for every naughty thing I ever did. I still think about that fire—and behave.

The cheese maker and his family lived in the same building, and the whole place reeked of curds and whey. Our last stop on our tour was the storeroom where the big wheels of cheese, covered in cheesecloth and wax, were stacked. I had a tremendous feeling of power standing among these towering remnants of our labor.

In the spring we went on a field trip to pick mayflowers. We traipsed through the gully and the last remnants of melting snow searching of trilliums, cowslips, and violets. Invariably, our trip ended when someone slipped into the creek. Lola usually had a droopy centerpiece for the supper table.

By the time Betty and I reached grade three, Iverson and Laura had graduated from high school and were starting their careers. Memories of my older siblings on the farm are sparse. Iverson attended Agricultural College after high school, and Laura went to Business College in the city and worked at Metropolitan Life. Then both joined the Air Force.

With her older children serving in the military and the twins off at school all day, Lola had more time to plant flowers, paint walls, make curtains, try new recipes, and design really great aprons. Sometimes she even took her apron off. But even bigger changes were in the wings for our first lady.

Electricity, Spam (the food), and Tide reached the Dell Farm at about the same time around 1945. Lola's step lightened and her aprons flared as she added more spice and flavor to life's bounty. Electricity revolutionized our existence. Inside the house, Mother Nature no longer controlled the light. Lola's day started when she chose to turn on the lights and ended when she chose to turn them off. In between she no longer had fires to tend, water to heat, lamp chimneys to clean, or lard to render.

Kitchen maintenance was cut in half: no wood chips to sweep, no smoke on the walls, no ashes to carry, and the string of unsightly stove pipes across the kitchen ceiling vanished. Lola was thinking about new linoleum. She used the flat irons for doorstops and abandoned the chamber pots for a running water commode. Lola had a bathroom to decorate.

On Monday morning she no longer had to pump water or stoke fires. An electric motor replaced the gas engine on the washing machine. New taps at the sink filled the machine and soapsuds rose from the hot water like clouds on a summer day. A handful of Tide worked miracles and lasted through the very last load. On Tuesday Lola spread the sheets on the big table, plugged in the iron, and sang as she slid the shiny chrome miracle over piece after piece without ever stopping to lick a finger.

Baking no longer started with building and stoking a fire. Lola could whip up a batch of biscuits on a whim and the sugar topping was always the perfect shade of brown. Now Lola was thinking built-in cabinets.

Lola found Spam sitting right there on the grocer's shelf. She had heard the stories from the war front—if it was good enough for our soldiers, she could certainly put it on her table. She reached for a can and then took another. On the way home she marveled at her good fortune; the possibilities were limitless. Meat for any meal cooked and preserved sitting on a kitchen shelf—just waiting—and she hasn't lifted a finger in its preparation. She put one can in the new refrigerator and the other in the pantry. One hot summer evening, Lola sliced fresh vegetables from the garden on a big platter lined with crisp leaf lettuce. Then she carved the chilled spam, very thin, and fanned it around the perimeter. She added a bowl of potato salad and supper was served. She offered fried Spam and eggs for breakfast one morning and then put Spam on her regular grocery list. Now Lola was thinking Hawaiian Spam.

In between the new linoleum, the built in cabinets, and decorating the new bathroom, Lola began sending food packages overseas to Iverson and to Laura on the home front. Then came the big news that Iverson was getting married—in England to an English girl. There was no thought of our family attending the wedding. Bombs were dropping on London, and even in peacetime, travel overseas was limited to a select few. But Lola would see that the family was properly represented. She counted ration stamps and collected pounds of candied fruit, almond paste, and icing sugar, and set about baking a rich fruit wedding cake. The three layers were baked to perfection in the electric oven. Then Lola packed them in two big square tin boxes and tucked the icing sugar, butter, and almond paste into crevices and corners. She sealed the tins by completely covering them in melted wax. I never knew exactly why they were waxed, but in my young, landlocked country mind, I figured it had something to do with crossing the ocean. The whole effort became very romantic as Iverson wrote about receiving the cake and strapping the two big boxes to the basket of a bicycle and peddling them to a local baker to assemble and ice for the wedding. Despite the fierce rationing in London, they had a very posh wedding. Their wedding photographs showed Iverson in his uniform and the bride in a long white satin gown (black market) cutting an impressive three-tier wedding cake.

    Our world was changing. The war was ending. Iverson was married. And Betty was menstruating. Lola walked into Hodgins' General Store and plunked down cash for the big set of dishes. Now she had enough china to set the big table—fully extended.

Lola's role changes

With the flick of a switch,

A box of Tide,

And a can of Spam.

Chapter 4 - Betty: The Tall One

At the White House:

Tall, slender, and graceful of figure, Mrs. Roosevelt presents herself to hold press conferences, travel, and give lectures and radio broadcasts. She had a daily syndicated newspaper column called *My Day*. She visited servicemen abroad during World War II.

At the Dell Farm:

Betty walks tall and presents herself as we travel through childhood.

B etty sat across the table, her chair turned to face the camera, her back straight; head held high, long legs touching at the knee—her left toe pointed directly at the lens. Her slim hand and long fingers visored one eye as she coyly surveyed the project at hand. She was four years old, and it was evident she was born to pose.

I sat at the same table and faced the same camera, short and scrunched up with one knee raised halfway to my chin—my panties showing. The developed picture showed twin girls having a tea party in the garden—a lush, healthy rhubarb plant in the background.

We wore the same skirts and sweaters. We shared the same parents and birthday. We looked into the same camera, but differences tell our stories.

Betty's twenty-minute head start in life and her inches of added height projected a superior status. Her clothes were one size larger than mine, her shoes longer and narrower, and her stockings hitched up smooth on her long legs. At night Mother set Betty's straight hair with rag curlers. Every morning Mother brushed our hair into the same style and tied it with ribbons the same color. By day's end my naturally curly hair was frizzy, my ribbon often stuffed in my panties pocket, and my stockings wrinkled down around my ankles.

Betty: Panty pockets were a wonderful idea. It was simpler to stitch a little patch pocket on the panties than to position them on a frilly dress. Summer dresses had matching panties. Fleece-lined panties, garter belts, and ribbed stockings were the dreaded winter attire.

The picture forecasted our lifestyle. Betty the tall one walked lofty and presented herself in a sophisticated manner. I, the little one, meandered and explored—rumpled and cute. From my birth to my marriage, Betty walked two steps ahead of me. We had grand adventures and petty disagreements as we traveled together through life. Signposts along our road read "playing house," "school lore," "clothes and hair," "chores," "boys," and "coming-of-age." Throughout our journey we made regular stops at the kitchen table to nourish our bodies, receive direction, and establish our status in life.

Betty sat on her little chair with a doll across her knee. She buttoned the back of the doll's dress, turned her over, and selected a wide blue ribbon to thread through the loop in her painted composition hair. Then she held Cora at arm's length and admired her doll child. I sat with Gertrude, a replica of Cora, and contemplated the hole in her head and how I wished I could make the deformity disappear without tying a ribbon on it. I plunked Gertrude in the chair, ribbonless, and set about laying the table for our dolls' breakfasts. I fussed with little pieces of fabric salvaged from under Lola's sewing machine—napkins for Cora and Gertrude. Betty and Cora waited patiently, icons with sleek hair and crisp bows.

Our play area on the upstairs' landing was home to six dolls, their beds, and our little table and two chairs. Sometimes we moved all or part of this miniature household to our outside summer playhouse or to the warmth of the kitchen. I set and reset our little table; a small china tea set was supplemented with an assortment of colorful jar lids. For grand make-believe occasions, Lola loaned us side plates and saucers. We were referred to as The Twins but Betty dominated the small-scale setting and was assumed in charge.

For large family celebrations, both the big table and our little table were set in the kitchen. The big table was spread with a linen cloth and set with the drab brown English china service from the china cabinet. Our little table was spread with an embroidered sugar bag tea cloth and set with our Bunnykins dishes by Royal Doulton. At the end of each day our play furniture was returned to the indoor upstairs area and we tucked our babies into their respective beds.

> *Betty on dolls: Cora and Gertrude were our constant companions. They fit very nicely into our outgrown clothes. Their ribbon head loop was fine with me. Without the loop how could they have a ribbon? Little girls wore ribbons.*

Pat and Pearl were rubber baby dolls. They were indestructible and survived time spent neglected outside in the rain and snow. With a bath and a fresh nightie, they were new again. We heard about the baby wet-ums dolls, listening to Santa Claus read children's Christmas wish letters on the radio. Most girls requested baby wet-ums and so we did, too. The premise was that water inserted into the mouth came out the other end, wetting the diaper. Our babes arrived under the Christmas tree and soon thereafter disaster struck. We sterilized the tiny pointed nipples in boiling water on the woodstove, turning them into a gummy blob.

Lola tucked us into bed. In the winter, hot water bottles awaited our cold feet and we cocooned in flannel sheets and patchwork quilts. We built an invisible fence down the middle of the bed and went through the motions of defending our separated territories. Betty had the advantage; her long legs snaked into distant spaces and blocked my futile advances. But this touching and squabbling added security to our warm nest.

Our preschool days revolved around three meals at the big table; play, indoors and out; ringlets, ribbons, and cookies. When we started to school, things changed.

The big kids huddled in groups, eyed us, and whispered. We wore identical clothes, had a shared lunch bag for recess, and we went home at noon for our afternoon nap. Mother told us that we were special. Betty knew we were special. She walked tall and out-strut the bullies. I followed close and tried to mimic her.

> *Betty's bit: I wasn't aware of being taller than you until we started school. Our teacher, Gwenyth Shaw, asked the class to*

sit up straight with feet flat on the floor. I was surprised and concerned that your feet wouldn't reach the floor. Would Miss Shaw punish you or tell Mom of your shortcoming?

When Miss Shaw sent a note home to say we were missing spelling class every afternoon, Lola rethought our afternoon nap, and we started attending school full-time. It did not take long for the other kids to accept us as normal.

For breakfast, the big table was set with our Bunnykins dishes. Lola helped us plan our day as she coaxed another spoon of porridge and spread our toast with jam or jelly. After breakfast we would take turns sitting on the high stool to have our hair fixed. For full-time school our ringlets were replaced with pigtails. Every hair had to be in place and our bows perky-perfect. On a few occasions, we missed our ride to school because all four pigtails were not finished—farmers didn't hold their horses while Lola tweaked pigtails.

Lunch with our schoolmates was a new experience. Lola packed a wonderful lunch topped with a folded cloth napkin. I took out my napkin and tucked it in at my neck. I heard the kids snicker. Betty deftly unfolded her napkin, slowly turned around, scanning each classmate, spread her napkin on her lap, straightened her back, crossed her long legs, and picked up her sandwich—her little finger pointing to the sky. Before the week ended all the girls were putting on airs—spreading their napkins.

When we got home in the afternoon Lola had a snack waiting for us. Sometimes we had a cookie and milk, but usually it was something leftover from the noon meal, pudding or a cold boiled potato slathered in butter and sprinkled with salt and pepper. My favorite snack was a ladle of soup from the big pot on the back of the stove. Whatever the treat, it was served in the appropriate dish at the big table. We tucked our napkins in at the neck and talked about our day as we showed Lola our school papers. Bran muffins, hot from the oven, were another one of my favorite snacks.

Betty: The lunch napkin was not just for protecting clothing and dabbing the mouth. Lunch was wrapped in the napkin. Our one source of waxed paper was the lining from dry cereal boxes and we rarely had dry cereal. I shudder thinking about the day my egg sandwich was packed in a bag that had brown sugar in it —the bread had turned orange and sweet.

Walking to school was an adventure. The road followed up and down hills, beside a fast moving creek, and past three homesteads. We dodged a chained dog and hissing geese. We walked on gravel or skied on snow. In summer the boys fished minnows from the creek with a worm impaled on a bent pin and tied to a string. In winter we looked forward to an enhanced ski jump on the big hill. We shared our walk with other children on their way to school. Most trips were made without encountering a vehicle.

Betty: We often walked to school with the Bean kids, Winona, Elburn, and Lyle. They lived about a quarter of a mile up the road and we would see them leave their home as we finished breakfast. The Stark farm was on the other side of our place and about halfway to school. On cold mornings we were welcomed into their kitchen to warm up by the stove. They had lots of kids and a few more trampling in with snowy boots didn't seem to be a problem.

We did well in school. Betty enjoyed class time and got the highest grades. My grades were okay. The best part of school was recess and lunch hour. We played games in the schoolyard, and in winter we skied or slid down the hill behind the school. Lots of kids skied to school and everyone helped pack trails and make ski jumps. Sleighs and toboggans were status symbols; they were the big boys' vehicles. This is where we learned to vie for the boy with the best toy. I was partial to Gordon Alexander's sloop sleighs. His sloops were designed to haul logs. They didn't handle well on the slopes, but they were shiny, bright red, and an oddity. I was thrilled to sit behind Gordie as he bogged down in the deep snow or was upset along the ski jump. Betty fancied Dolton Elliott: he played guitar and sang, but his toboggan promised adventure. She wrapped her arms around Dalton's waist and held on too tight as they flew over the ski jump. Betty loved to make an impression.

> Betty: I didn't enjoy the school skating rink. Water was carried in pails from the cheese factory and dumped on packed snow in the yard. I couldn't skate and hated rink days. Mother said it was because I had weak ankles and I was happy to have that for an excuse.

Lola lamented, "I don't understand why twin sisters argue so much." Dad responded by promising us each a wristwatch if we didn't bicker for one month. I don't remember arguing but we must have. I do remember biting my tongue when Betty's watch had gold minute dots and mine didn't. I suspect we argued about dressing alike and our clothes.

Clothes became more and more important. Other kids bragged about their new clothes from the catalogue and made apologies for their homemade items. For Betty and me, Lola's designs were superior, and clothes from the catalogue more common and poorly sized. Betty cared for her clothes. She hung them up properly, and smoothed her skirt before she sat down. When beige jackets and dark brown skirts were the rage, we ordered jackets from the catalogue and Lola made us skirts. One day, on my way home from school, I took a shortcut through a cow pasture and hung my new jacket on a fence post before climbing through barbwire. When I got back the next day to retrieve my blazer, a calf had chewed off one elbow. We could not discard two brand new jackets because of my carelessness, so the elbow was darned. I tried rolling up my sleeve and tying a bandanna around my elbow while Betty strutted into class every day in her perfect beige and brown outfit.

> Betty adds: During the war when Iverson was overseas, Dad said he needed our help with the milking chores and we would be paid $2.00 a week. The red, box-style, wool coats featured in the winter catalogue for $18.00 could now be ours. We saved the money and ordered the coats. They were more beautiful than described— lined with a luxurious red quilted slippery material.

Chores were a part of daily life; setting the table, doing the dishes, and bringing in wood were regular household duties. In summer we were on standby to help harvest fruit and vegetables when they reached their peak. We were also called on to help with cattle and field maintenance if regular hands were busy with the harvest.

We were paid for some chores. Strawberries were our biggest cash crop: we made five cents for each basket we picked. With money this easy, we were prone to over-pick. When we did, Lola got on the party line to find customers for the extra berries, and if she did not find anyone, she made more strawberry jam. I suspect Betty is doing penance for our excess picking when she continues to makes strawberry jam every summer.

Other chores merited a special treat. One hot summer day Dad promised to take us to the bay (Sand Bay) to swim after supper if we helped fill the silo. The silo was filled with chopped-up corn plants mixed with molasses; this silage needed to be tramped around the edges to prevent air pockets. Swimming in the evening sounded very worldly, so Betty and I climbed into the silo and did the side step around its circumference all day long. When we washed up at the end of our workday, we were horrified to find our feet stained dark brown from the molasses. We quickly pulled on our socks and shoes. Betty figured out how we could get in the water without anyone seeing our feet. Grandpa's rowboat was nosed up on shore, and we sat in the back and took off our shoes and socks then slipped over the stern into a foot of water. Betty was good at working out details. We enjoyed our treat for a hard day's work.

> *Betty: I thoroughly enjoyed being assigned the task of picking up the large stones that the plowing operation turned up. We had a tractor, a wagon, and a big field. How grown-up was that —unsupervised with such valuable equipment? I was less enthused about the daily chore of getting the cows to pasture at the other farm. We traveled through the gully and across one field to reach the road leading to the gate at the Upper Place. Not as simple as it sounds. If we didn't keep them moving at a good pace they might wander up lanes into neighboring yards or a barking dog might scare them off in the wrong direction. When our cows got mixed up with the neighbor's herd it caused much confusion and sorting out.*

One year when all the young men were away at war, Betty and I did extra duty at harvest time and received an extra-special treat. We each got a one-week luxury vacation at Great-Aunt Margaret's posh city apartment. I enjoyed the adventure of being in the city on my own but I did not like being totally responsible; I missed Betty's direction.

Grandpa Charlie's cottage at Sand Bay was a special childhood haunt. Our city aunts and uncles came to the cottage for their summer vacation. The cousins who were our age wanted to spend time at the Dell Farm while Betty and I longed to spend time at the cottage. It was at the cottage that we saw how our city kin lived. The women wore slacks and shorts; Lola put on her church dress to go to the cottage. Their cupboards were full of cans and cardboard boxes; ours held jars of preserves and tin boxes full of baked goods. Their meat was cut into fancy chops and steaks; we had roasts. They sat down at the table to eat three meals each day like we did, but they served meals at different times. The colorful place settings were most impressive: each setting was a different color. Some aunts mixed these colors up so each person had four or five different colors—bright, fun, and perfect for Grandpa's cottage. It was (and still is) called Fiesta and Betty decided she must have Fiesta for her table.

There were big changes at the Dell Farm. Electricity and prepared food made life easier. Betty and I were growing up. We had new hairstyles, went to our first dance, and anticipated our monthly period. We cut our hair; both choosing bangs. Betty gave herself a home permanent; now we both had frizzy hair. We looked just like the Toni Twins in the new advertisements.

One of the Bean boys was home from the war and getting married. The reception invitation read, "Tom, Lola, Betty, & Barbara." Lola showed us the invitation and told us there would be dancing and that we could go. We were dumbfounded. Without consulting Great-Aunt Margaret, Lola ordered dresses from the catalogue. She picked a rust-colored crepe, draped across the bodice with a flounce down one side. Betty and I agreed on the featured new style: mustard-colored gabardine with cap sleeves and a keyhole neckline outlined with silver nail heads. I had never danced and was quite apprehensive. Betty told me not to worry; that no one would ask us to dance—but she was wrong. Two of the Bean boys—there were seven of them—asked us to square dance, and we were pulled, pushed, and swung around the big kitchen. I bumped into the fiddle player and lost one of my nail heads.

Betty swirled her full skirt and do-si-doed. Lola clapped in time to the music. Tom tapped his right foot. The war was ending and times were good. But Great-Aunt Margaret would not have appreciated this country wedding.

World War II spins off new products and new technology, but it took both the First and the Second World Wars to produce sanitary products and get them (still wrapped in plain brown paper) on the shelf at the general store. Army nurses in World War I discovered that cellulose-wrapped bandages made great feminine protection. After the war, a surplus of bandage material was converted to Kotex. But superstition and stigma made marketing this liberating product virtually impossible. A breakthrough came during World War II when Kimberly-Clark introduced advertisements in support of the war effort. Their ad encouraged young women to join the Cadet Nurse Corps and keep going in comfort by choosing Kotex products.

Mother showed Betty and me where a giant box of sanitary pads was hidden—away in the back of an upstairs closet. Then she sat us down to talk and gave us each one of the new sanitary belts

> *Betty remembers: Mom produced for our enlightenment a little booklet that had arrived weeks earlier in the mailbox. It was titled "Just Between Us." She read this to us, or with us, adding a few personal comments and cautions. It contained some pictures and diagrams that were briefly and delicately introduced.*

My sanitary belt was a powerful symbol of womanhood and I could not wait to use it. I snuck it under the covers at night and tried it on. As usual, Betty started her period first and proudly strapped on her sanitary belt.

> *Betty's laments: In my experience the sanitary belt was a total failure. It kept sliding off my hips. Prior to resorting to anchoring the pad to my drawers with a couple of safety pins, I was sent to deliver an urgent message to our father operating equipment in a distant field. I ran the whole way with my knees together to keep from losing my harness.*

Finally, while at summer camp, I had my period and with it a profound feeling of self-awareness—something very personal that I didn't have to immediately share with Betty. A letter written from Girl Scout camp delivered my news to Mother. My letter, like the one in the china cabinet, is private—my business. I am a woman. When I arrived home Mother and I sipped tea from fancy china cabinet cups. I belonged to a new club, a club that Betty had joined months before. But I was the new member and the center of attention.

Betty's response: Barbara, you have remembered the event very dramatically. For me the entire puberty thing is a bit of a blur. I recall pink spotting on new fleece-lined underwear. No "Whoo, I'm a Woman" rush. I was eleven years old. Between the worry of getting the cows to and from the Upper place each day and having to catch and ride that damn horse, my stomach was already cramped up. Who needed more belly discomfort?

Betty and I were born a pair. As we made the transition to womanhood, we experienced signs of separation. We dressed differently, had separate beds, and were no longer referred to as The Twins. We had different haircuts and new place settings. Our Bunnykins' dishes were moved from the kitchen cupboard to the china cabinet, ready for the next generation of children. For special occasions, the big table was set with the familiar, and somewhat faded, white and brown English china. Lola's new, made-in-Japan settings brighten our everyday table. But we had discovered Fiesta Ware. Its bold new colors offered a wonderful counterbalance to the difficult and bleak war years. As World War II ended, our brother took over the farm. His wife ran the house and we moved to town.

> Betty and I reach womanhood
> With new responsibilities
> And freedom to set our table
> In a bold new way.

Chapter 5 - The Englishwoman Upsets the Tea Cart

At the White House:

From 1948-1952, The White House underwent major renovations. The natural oak paneling in the dining room was painted a soft green popularly called Williamsburg green. First Lady Bess Truman selects china with the same shade of green.

At the Same Time:

Major renovations take place at the Dell Farm.

T he picture was skewed. Familiar characters were in new roles. There were unfamiliar gestures, missing symbols and foreign sounds; and a new woman was in the kitchen.

Our family sat around the big table; guests were in the house. Everyone was twitching. Dad rolled his thumbs. The Englishwoman—big, bold, and beautiful—was washing diapers in the kitchen sink. Upstairs in what was my bedroom, a baby cried. The new woman bounded up the stairs, a wet diaper trailing from her hand. There was water on the new linoleum. Her name was Pat and she was my brother, Iverson's, war bride and she had no idea how to run a house.

Dad waited impatiently in the car with Betty. Mother lagged behind with her gift for the baby. The night before she had taken Iverson's baby spoon from the china cabinet, polished it, wrapped it in a crocheted doily, and tied it with a blue ribbon. Now she was giving it to the Englishwoman for baby Lindsay, Lola's first grandchild.

I felt like Dorothy dropped into the Land of Oz. I was the one designated to introduce the Englishwoman to the farm and help her settle into the house. This was my first womanly assignment. I found a mop and wiped up the water. My first evening with the Englishwoman was amazing: she sang *I've Got a Lovely Bunch of Coconuts*, asked my brother to knock her up at seven, and smoked cigarettes. I liked her.

We unpacked crate after crate of wonderful place settings, silver, crystal, brass, and dozens of teacups. Then we opened boxes looking for cookbooks. The barn raisers were coming. We had a table to set and pies to make. I opened a cookbook and found measurements in pounds and ounces. We didn't have a scale. Pat confessed, "I've never made pastry." I volunteered to make the pastry, but I didn't know about the filling. Pat looked through the cupboards and came up with two boxes of raisins saying, "I've watched my mother make currant turnovers." To which I responded, "I have watched my mother make most every kind of pie—except raisin."

I lined two pie plates with pastry. Pat sang and bounced the baby on one hip as she poured a box of raisins into each shell, sprinkled them generously with brown sugar and dotted them with big blobs of butter. Then she directed me to "top 'em off." I rolled on the top crust, crimped, slit, and popped two pies in the oven with the roast.

I peeled the vegetables and Pat set the table. She placed two little silver salt sellers with teeny-weeny spoons on the table: I hadn't seen salt sellers before. Pat explained that they were individual and each place should have one. She only had two so they had to share. She knew how to set a proper table.

The new woman of the house wiped baby spit from the front of her frock as the men arrived for dinner. Her jovial mood put them at ease as they sat down at the big table. Bert Stark asked if he could help, and Pat plunked Baby Lindsay on his knee. Bert had a houseful of children and was right at home with the baby. The men filled their plates. One lifted a salt seller, took the little spoon out, emptied the salt onto his plate and used the little spoon to stir the salt into his potatoes and gravy.

Pat cut the pies as I removed the empty plates. She picked up the baby and set the first piece of pie in front of Bert saying, "Try this. I don't think it's quite right." His expression froze as he poked around in the pie with his fork. "You've made buck-shot pie," he proclaimed. I got rid of the little pellets and pastry mess. Pat emptied two bags of store-bought cookies (she called them biscuits) into a big cut-glass bowl and passed them around the table.

As the men left the table, Bert told Pat he would come the next morning and show her how to make raisin pie. My brother, who had sat throughout dinner with a weird grin on his face, hugged his wife. I had played a bit part in Pat's premier performance.

It was four o'clock in the afternoon and the adventure continued as we walked through the barnyard (no yellow brick—just mud). I was all dressed up in my white eyelet dress. I held up one end of a giant silver tray laden with china cups and two lovely teapots. Pat sang out, "Tea time."

The hammering stopped. Iverson stood one foot on each side of the peak. Like the Jolly Giant he surveyed the scene below and quipped, "Well, lads, I guess we should get down off this roof and have us a tea party."

Before the sun set that evening, every woman in the county knew that the Englishwoman smoked, didn't know how to make pie, and served tea in the barnyard; but this new woman had already expanded their horizons and she was destined to champion their changing roles. The postwar boom propelled her with new technology, new products, happy music, and a new set of wheels.

Bert Stark, true to his word, taught Pat how to make raisin pie. He also showed her how to make bread pudding and seven minute icing. Pat was a quick study. She collected cookbooks with measurements in cups and spoons and bought a kitchen scale for her English recipes. Her table featured steak and kidney pie and the farm's traditional roast, great currant turnovers, and the English version of Lola's famous coconut cream pie. She discovered more prepared foods on the grocer's shelf and tried every recipe on the side of the newly available boxed cake mix. The development of the aerosol can allowed us to add a quick dab of whipped cream to life's goodies.

The big round table was replaced by a trendy, red chrome set to match the new linoleum. For family meals the table was set with placemats, and the place settings were Melamine in a bright plaid pattern: plastic dishes on a plastic table. For company meals, an Irish linen cloth was spread and the table was set with Original Bridal Rose, the china Pat had brought from England.

The red chrome table was set three times a day and attracted not only tradesmen and farm workers, but new friends from town.

The farmers enjoyed gathering at Pat's table. The food was good and the table was set with old-world charm. Pat sang and thought nothing of involving the men in the meal's preparation. She also attracted young couples from town to her table. These guests often spent the weekend, helped with the chores, and played cards into the wee hours. Pat was the first to introduce us to the new Argentine card game called Canasta.

Wartime clothing shortages disappeared and stores started offering markdowns and new fabrics. New dress material needed little ironing. Pat hung clothes on the umbrella clothesline to drip-dry, and we used the new ironing board less and less.

She knit but she didn't sew; so when Lola gave her one of the new zigzag sewing machines, she passed it along to her mother. Dad thought this was irresponsible.

Lola's eyes sparkled, and she stifled a grin as they watched Pat drive up in her shiny new black sedan. She talked about buying groceries and running errands, but she was probably thinking about afternoon Canasta with the girls and joining the curling team. Wheels set her free to explore new interests. At the same time the first jet airliner flew out of London and domestic airlines lowered fares as a step toward affordable mass air transportation. Pat thought about visiting family in England.

Communications got faster. Pat's letters were addressed to London, England, and no doubt contained very personal revelations and confessions about life in her new world. Our rural postman picked up her Air Letter (a single sheet of paper folded into a stamped envelope with red and blue slashes around the edge). I wondered if letters flown across the ocean received the same respect and confidentiality we afforded the old letter in our china cabinet.

The party-line telephone came off the wall and a cradle phone sat on the sideboard. The first long-distance dial telephone call connected New York and San Francisco in just twelve seconds.

Pat made the transition from the heart of London to the rural Dell Farm by transforming her new environment wherever she saw fit. Walls came down, some of them one brick at a time. She was the talk of the Corner when she bundled up the baby and joined her husband in the evening at the all-male sit in at the country store. Iverson minded the baby while she swept stones at the curling rink. She drove 125 miles into the city to shop at the Fat Ladies Shop and have her hair done. She didn't wear a corset.

Other walls came down in one fell swoop. The partitions for Great-Aunt Margaret's room were torn down to enlarge the parlor. The piano went with us to town and Pat replaced it with a combination radio/record player that played the new seven-inch 45 rpm record. Shelves went up on one wall to display brass animals from England. Feather pillows softened the seating. "Zip-a-Dee-Doo-Dah" and "Smoke, Smoke, Smoke (That Cigarette)" infused the parlor, referred to as the living room. Propriety was enlarged and entertainment expanded.

Upstairs the wall between what used to be Mum and Dad's room and Betty's and my room came down. Pat slept with the Farmer of the Dell in their master suite: secure and without inhibitions, thanks to new methods of contraception.

What used to be a six-bedroom house was now a three-bedroom house. The red plastic table was set three times a day and the kitchen was still the hub of the house; but all the rooms were accessible, spacious, colorful, and full of song.

The Englishwoman took The Corner by storm. Roles changed and our world expanded. I moved to town and attended high school.

> Dell Farm under new management.
> High Tea in the barnyard.
> Canasta at the kitchen table.

Chapter 6 - Our First Dining Room: The First McDonald's

At the White House:

Bess Wallace Truman did not welcome the position of First Lady. She kept social life to a minimum. A new American china State service was purchased during the Truman administration in 1951 from B. Altman & Co., New York City (made by Lenox China).

At the Same Time:

We moved to town and our social life exploded.

J ust like Cinderella, Lola, Betty, and I were whisked from the farm to the center of town. We were budding socialites in sugar bags. Dad was elected mayor and the weekly newspaper tagged him "The Barnyard Senator." Great-Aunt Margaret was recruited to oversee the protocol of our new social status.

    Our house was charming with good bones—a brick bungalow with double-decker sunrooms on the front. The kitchen was a fraction of the size of the farm kitchen and too small to be the center of activity. There were common rooms that offered choices for gathering, entertaining, and squatting. Lola was ecstatic to have a formal dining room off the kitchen where we would take all our meals. A small den with a fireplace provided an intimate setting for writing letters, winter chats, and summer naps, and provided spillover space from the large living room. Off the living room in the front, the sunroom was our summer retreat, complete with a squeaky, padded swing and a view of the sidewalk traffic. These rooms and two first-floor bedrooms boasted polished crown moldings and swinging French doors.

    The second floor was my special spot. A room as large as the farm kitchen was sunk into the rafters. A continuous row of hinged windows encircled the room at shoulder-height. The sunroom opened off the front. It was our solarium, penthouse, and tree house—posh accommodations for the mayor's daughters.

> *Betty's bit: The house was every bit as wonderful as you have described it, but have you forgotten what it didn't have? A bathroom! There was running water to the kitchen sink, and there may have been a tap in the basement laundry area, but that was it. Before Aunt Margaret arrived for her inspection tour, Dad had squeezed a bathroom into a storage area and a rather tiny shower was installed in our upstairs quarters.*

Great-Aunt Margaret walked around taking inventory. She opened doors and drawers and stopped in different spots to peruse the possibilities. She made lists and established priorities.

The china cabinet from the farm was the only functional piece of furniture in the dining room. A new dining suite went to the top of the shopping list. The windows were measured for new draperies, and the women of the house measured each other for afternoon and social dresses.

Auntie oversaw the delivery of the new dining room furniture. Soft, thick woven drapes were hung; they were pink to match the hedge of peonies outside. As Lola transferred pieces from the old china cabinet to the new sideboard, she pondered Aunt Margaret's suggestion, "Lola, you really should consider a new, more formal, china service. Your Johnson Brothers service is dull and missing many pieces, and your new yellow and red service is kitchenware. I recommend Staffordshire, Barratts of Balmoral. The burgundy and gold pattern will add drama." Mother smiled, picked up the old letter, and talked to herself, saying, "I will set the highest standard." Then she coyly slipped the letter into her apron pocket.

Lola was thrilled as she stacked and displayed the new china service. She cut a big bunch of peonies, arranged them in the cut-glass water pitcher, and placed them on the new table. Then she sat down with a nice cup of tea and wallowed in the ambiance of her first dining room.

I wondered where she put the old letter.

Our presence was requested at baby showers, teas, and church socials. Lola made fancy tea aprons and served tea and little sandwiches in the dining room, lemonade and cookies on the sun porch, and coffee and cake in the living room. It was as if she were born to entertain.

There was a small, two-seat breakfast nook in the kitchen; but, even when there were only two for dinner, Lola set the dining room table. The breakfast nook had placemats and the dining room table was spread with a pad and a lace cloth. A mirrored centerpiece reflected the choice of the moment from the china cabinet.

Betty and I immersed ourselves in our new environment, but we had the "teenage thing" happening as well—poodle skirts, angora sweaters, hooded coats, saddle shoes, and boys consumed our thoughts. For the first time we were allowed to dress differently. We received $8.00 a month as a clothing allowance. I sewed and knit. A dollar bought the yardage for a dress, and it took two dollars to buy the yarn for one of the new baggy sweaters. When dress lengths changed, I lengthened skirts by adding a contrasting flounce or inserting a wide sash. Old sweaters were unraveled and knit into new patterns. I enjoyed the recreating process.

Betty adds: I knit, too, but sewing was not my forte. I was intimidated by the speed of our new electric sewing machine. Mrs. Barr, next door, said I could use her treadle machine, but Mum didn't think that was a good idea, so all sewing was done in-house. Mum sewed for free and Barbara would 'run up' a dress for $2.00.

Traditionally we were not given gifts on our birthday; but on our sixteenth birthday, Mum bought us each a good hairbrush and a satin slip—tools for womanhood.

We had to earn money for nonessentials like cokes and lipstick. I baby-sat; the going rate varied with the customer. Sometimes I received as much as fifty cents an hour. Betty worked at the telephone switchboard. She earned 10 cents an hour, but she had a steady schedule and employment. A coke cost five cents and a lipstick less than a dollar.

Betty elaborates: I thought being a telephone operator was a very grown-up position. It was something I could put on my resume. I also had regular babysitting clients, and Dad would pay us for jobs over and above the regular daily chores we were expected to do. A car wash was good for movie money and cleaning out the cistern, a big dirty job, might fund a school sweater.

The school was at the dead end of our street and the sidewalk passed in front of our house. We walked home for lunch. I liked it when Mum set a small table on the sun porch. This allowed me to keep tabs on who left school to go to Mrs. Pappin's snack shop; and when they started back to school, I popped into the entourage beside whichever boy I currently fancied.

Betty comments: I loved living in town. No cows to collect or horse to worry about, no more trudging through waist-high snow drifts to school. On the coldest day, I went to school in bobby socks; no need to bundle up in heavy ugly clothing. We could wait at home until the bell rang and manage to get to school before the doors closed.

At sixteen neither of us had, or were permitted to have, a boyfriend, but it was time to start filling our hope chest. A cedar chest in the spare bedroom was the depository for embroidered pillowcases, tea cloths and napkins—some were made from sugar bags. Mother contributed wonderful quilts she designed, pieced, and needle worked. Aunts and friends added crocheted and tatted lace, teacups, cake plates, and pieces for our silverware pattern. Betty and I had no problem keeping our items separate - we had very different tastes and color preferences.

There was controversy over career education and summer jobs. Dad stressed the need for us to have a marketable skill—what would we do if our husbands died and left us with a slew of kids to bring up? There was no advanced training available locally, Mother thought we were too young to go off on our own, and Betty and I had different career aspirations. After many nights of pleading our cases, arguing, cajoling, and crying, Dad put his foot down and said, "You must agree on the same training and you must decide in the next twenty-four hours." There was no encouragement to follow our passion and no assurance that we could be anything we wanted to be—career training was survival insurance.

Betty and I decided on business school. We reasoned that typing, shorthand, and penmanship would open up different positions for our consideration. Mother made a long-distance phone call and arranged for us to stay with our sister Laura and her husband Chuck, who lived near several business schools.

Betty and I and our friend June found a help-wanted ad for summer jobs at Red Deer Lodge, a resort near Grandfather Charlie's cottage. We fantasized about all the money we would make and the interesting city people we might meet. We didn't think our parents would let as apply, but we decided to try. We approached Mother first. We explained our need for long winter coats to cover our new longer skirts. We knew we could earn enough money to buy coats and provide spending money to carry us through the winter. When Mother made inquiries about our accommodations at the lodge and then agreed to talk to Dad, we knew we had a "go."

At Red Deer Lodge we were assigned guests by cabin number, and we looked after all their needs for the duration of their stay. We knew the potential for a big tip when they left. My strategy was to provide wonderful table settings. I picked wild flowers and gathered leaves and pinecones to accent the plain white cloth and dishes. We used our midafternoon break to lie on the beach and work on a tan. After we served the evening meal, we hung out or went to local dances. It was at one of these dances that I met Lee Palmer. The rest of the summer we kept bumping into each other. I had a boyfriend.

Betty spills the beans: Away from home and on our own for the first time, we worked and played hard that summer. In addition to our regular responsibilities at the lodge, we were encouraged to socialize with the guests. We played games, fetched drinks, and prepared snacks. The men flirted with us and tipped well. And when there was a dance within a twenty-mile radius we somehow got there. We didn't lie on the beach just to get a tan. We were exhausted. We slept and tanned. If our parents had known how we traveled around the county and the hours we kept, we would have been locked up.

When the summer ended we went home to get ready for business school. I didn't expect to see Lee again. He lived an hour away by car, and he didn't have a car. I was soon leaving for Laura's house halfway across the country.

We ordered our winter coats from the catalogue. Mine was a double-breasted maroon greatcoat, fitted with a half belt. The ad promised a more interesting "walkaway" look. Betty's was a dramatic brown, flared style with a hood. Both measure twelve inches from the floor. I made a maroon plaid beret and a matching long straight skirt - there was nothing like a good coat to anchor one's winter wardrobe.

Before we left for Laura's, two big firsts happened. Our family had dinner in a restaurant, and my boyfriend had dinner at our house. There was no restaurant in our small town. A snack bar offered hamburgers and hotdogs and a place for teenagers to hang out. Restaurants in larger towns and cities were patronized by travelers. It was not the custom to eat out instead of eating at home. But across the country in California, the McDonald brothers opened a hamburger stand—the burgers were fifteen cents, soft drinks ten cents, and coffee five cents. This fast-food eatery attracted busy professionals and students.

Dad often took the family on Sunday afternoon drives through the country. One Sunday when it was getting late and we were complaining about being hungry, Dad pulled into the Dew Drop Inn. He turned to Mother and said, "How about we eat supper out tonight?" Mother must have been in on the plan because she didn't question the cost or worry about perfectly good food going to waste at home. The food and the table setting didn't hold a candle to dinner in our new dining room, but we enjoyed ordering from a menu and being served food we didn't prepare at a table we didn't set. We all ordered hamburger steak - a welcome change from the roasts and chops at home.

The Sunday before we were to leave for business school, a strange car rattled into our driveway. Lee stepped out smiling from ear to ear. He waved and sauntered to the front of the car, lifted the hood, made an adjustment, and the engine shut down. Then he loudly announced, "I bought a car so I could see you before you head out west." I reluctantly introduced him to Mother and Dad. Betty whispered, "Now you're in trouble." We couldn't go for a drive because there was just enough gas to get Lee back home, so we sat on the side step and talked. I enjoyed the attention, but I felt like a stranger in my skin. Mother came out to say, "Supper will be ready in about twenty minutes. Will you eat with us, Lee?" I wanted to say that he would not, but he quickly accepted Mother's invitation. Mother tried to break the ice by asking about Lee's family. This didn't work—his mother and father were dead, he didn't know where one of his six brothers lived, and he was staying with an elderly aunt who was nothing like Great-Aunt Margaret. Then Dad took charge of the conversation and gave him advice on how to maintain his car. I think the car was beyond maintenance and wished everyone would stop talking, eat up, and get this ordeal over with. Boyfriends were not supposed to be invited for supper—I was not supposed to have a boyfriend. I felt abandoned. I started this journey in a broken-down car to a strange new land and everyone just waved goodbye.

Mother and Dad drove us across the country to Laura's house. She lived on the second floor of an old Victorian style house on the outskirts of the city. Betty and I were billeted in a large closet off her kitchen, a far cry from our spacious penthouse quarters at home. Before Mother left for home, she gave Laura a book and asked her to talk to us about sex. Laura was now responsible for both our business education and our sex education.

> *Betty remembers: There was no need for parental concern at this location. We had all winter to recover from our summer at the lodge. There was a large department store across from our school where I spent most lunch hours looking at all the wonderful displays, and watching people. Social life was nil. Our weekend treat was to go to the local snack bar, chat with the attendant, and suck on a coke for a couple of hours.*

Our time with Laura and at business school was an exercise in survival. Laura was expecting their second child, Chuck was working on a degree in theology, and Betty and I traveled thirty miles each day to and from school. During the evenings, we ate supper at a table squeezed into the stair landing. After supper Chuck would announce,

"It's time for devotions, girls." Everything stopped for devotions. The rest of the evening I sat on my cot in the closet and did homework, wrote letters, and knit a sweater to give Lee for Christmas.

Success Business College sent a monthly report home to parents. I wrote home weekly and Mother wrote back. Penmanship was critiqued during the process, and my spelling was always a subject of concern. Thank goodness there was no access to a typewriter for personal use and that Mother couldn't read shorthand. Long-distance phone calls were a luxury we didn't consider. I don't remember using the telephone while I was at Laura's.

When our college term ended, Laura and Chuck traveled home with us. Laura gave birth, Chuck worked with Dad for the summer, and we applied for work in the city. We traveled home by train—a luxury mode of travel. It took three days and two nights.

> *Betty was optimistic: I had not been on a train overnight and was amazed that we each had a bed at night that became a comfortable chair during the day. There was a tiny private washroom. After all those months away, I was excited to go home. I had a diploma from a first-rate business college. Everything was possible. Life would be good.*

It was so good to be home. Betty and I joked about all the wide-open space in our upstairs quarters. Mother bought an old typewriter and had all the neighbors in to watch us type. Mrs. Barr was amazed that we put in commas and periods. Mother prepared all our favorite foods and set picture-perfect tables in our grand dining room—a far cry from Laura's table on the stair landing.

> *Laura elaborates: Nobody could have labeled me a gracious hostess. I was content with basic and serviceable. Perhaps I can attribute this to life's journey: The Great Depression, the mess hall, living in remote areas, and moving more times than I can remember. My decor has always leaned more toward "Early Halloween" and my table settings are "Current Miscellany."*

I had one week to nestle in the comforts of home before I found myself filling out job applications. I'm not sure how I arrived at the huge bank that dealt in foreign exchange, but there I was—filing. Betty was employed in an office upstairs in the same building. She had a more prestigious position, probably because she was taller and had a more mature stature. Our pay was the same, $100 paid on the last day of each month.

I was seventeen, working and independent, free from adult supervision. I assumed full responsibility for my being, with no expectation of assistance. We found two more girls, and the four of us rented an apartment for $100 a month. On payday I put $25 in the rent pot, $25 in the food kitty, bought a book of streetcar tickets (transportation to work), and two bus tickets home. I had $30 left for personal needs.

> *Betty disputes my independence: Yes, you were clever to do so much with so little. But your claim to independence with no expectation of assistance is a bit of a stretch. I know firsthand that you weren't above bumming streetcar tickets and hitching a ride home on weekends. Mom provided wonderful care packages to take back to the city— lots of home-baked goodies; shampoo bottles were topped off and we helped ourselves to everything from toothpaste to shoe laces. We always got much love, advice, and support from the home front.*

Thirty dollars a month offered exciting possibilities—perhaps more than Great-Aunt Margaret spent on her personal pampering. I enjoyed making lists and prioritizing my expenditures. A tailored business suit was at the top of my list and choosing a china pattern was near the bottom. Before I received my first paycheck, eyeglasses ($25.00) had replaced the suit. The suit went back to the top of the next month's list. I watched the sales in all the good shops. It took two months, but I found the perfect suit for $27.00. It was a tailored gabardine in emerald green with a double-breasted jacket. The long pencil-slim skirt was slit up the back to the knee.

I took a streetcar to work and back to the apartment each weekday. Sometimes I stayed in the city after work for shopping or a movie. The night before payday the grocery budget was usually depleted and the four of us often shared a pack of cookies and a tin of pork and beans, but we set the table and shared our day. On weekends I alternated between going home and dating Lee in the city. Occasionally, Lee ended up at Mother's table for Sunday supper. I still lacked self-confidence when I presented Lee to my parents. I felt as if I was using a counterfeit $100 bill to buy a designer gown—I expected it to be questioned.

Weekends in the city were a fantasy world. My friends and co-workers all assumed Lee and I would get married. I played the part like Elizabeth Taylor. I was on a treadmill to stardom, and it was moving too fast to even think about stepping off.

Christmas Eve a fire burned in the fireplace, and bubbling candles lit up the Christmas tree. Lola had thought of everything—crystal candy dishes full of homemade fudge, dark and light fruitcakes, nuts, fruit; and a turkey was being stuffed in the kitchen. The silver was polished and candelabras sat on the dining room table. A snowstorm blew outside. The doorbell rang and Lola remarked, "I wonder who is out in this storm?" I answered the door and there stood Lee.

We sat in the cold car with the snow blowing through the window cracks. I looked down at the diamond on my finger and tears ran down my cheeks. What would I do now? I took the ring off my finger, tucked it into my pocket, and sent Lee home in the snowstorm. I promised to tell my parents about the ring the next week. Christmas remained intact. I announced my engagement to my parents in a letter. I picked November as the month I would marry—I would be eighteen in October and would no longer need parental consent. I was amazed and somewhat disillusioned when Mum and Dad offered no resistance to my wedding plans.

I put my ring on my finger and started making lists. I chose my wedding gown and veil, going-away suit, hat and purse, and used lay-away for making payments. I selected yardage for four attendant gowns—rich satin in jewel and fall colors that would reflect the candlelight at our twilight service. I spent more and more time after work scouting out the department stores looking for the perfect items at a price I could afford. Choosing a china pattern was problematic; I wanted a formal pattern, and I needed something suitable for casual settings.

I tucked the receipt for the next to last payment on my wedding gown in my purse. As I started toward the elevator I allowed my eyes to scan the lingerie department. There it was—the red satin housecoat that would forever haunt my fantasies: I sipped champagne in it, I lounged on satin pillows in it, I sprawled on a straw stack in it, I undid the top button to expose my small, firm breasts. I danced, letting the full circle skirt swoop like the jet stream, and I set the perfect table and served breakfast in it. That red satin robe would make any room or any event sumptuous; but like the china pattern, it was formal and I needed casual. The price tag was prohibitive; it read $39.95.

The wedding invitations were sent, the attendants' dresses made, my wedding dress was steamed and hung in the spare bedroom closet. Shower and wedding gifts piled up in the dining room and the den: linen, china, crystal, tea towels, potholders, and small appliances. Then the gift arrived that stole the show: white translucent Shelly china covered in rosebuds. I fell in love with the exquisite little teapot. My china pattern was decided—formal.

Dad said, "Straighten up and walk tall." The freezing rain had dampened my beautiful dress, and when I slipped on the church steps, I started to cry. Dad's stern words and the sudden crescendos to the wedding march jolted me back to the performance at hand.

The church doors opened and the candlelight scene set the stage. Pews adorned with Lily-of-the-Valley and candles marked rows of ladies' hats bobbing in the flickering light. Betty, in apricot satin, lead me to an array of Northern Lights reflecting from my attendants' satin gowns and bonnets as they arched my entrance—compelling proof of the ritual at hand.

Great-Aunt Margaret smiled from above.

> Our first dining room.
> The first McDonalds.
> My first china service.

Chapter 7 - My Home: My Table

At the White House:

The large Truman service had only been in use one year when the Eisenhower's came to the White House, so there was no valid reason to order another state dinner service. First Lady Mamie Eisenhower contributed to the White House china collection when she ordered 120 service plates, 11 ½ inches in diameter, at a cost of $3,606.40. The entire rim of each porcelain plate was covered with pure coin gold. First Lady Jacqueline Kennedy used the Truman china with the Eisenhower service plates for state dinners

At the Same Time:

Barbara sets her first table in the west wing of the Palmer house.

Like my ancestor who stowed the crystal knife rests in her canoe to later put on her table in the new world, I stepped into a new environment—I had a flannel bathrobe in my suitcase and boxes of fine china for my table. I intended to have a red satin dressing gown.

I laughed as Lee scooped me up and carried me over the threshold. Our threshold was a board on the floor in the hall—a crack in the floor. We had no door. Our living quarters amounted to three upstairs rooms in the west wing of the Palmer's house—no dining room, no red satin gown, and no door.

We had new furniture. We ordered it from the catalog. The closest furniture store was forty miles away. The pieces we chose were modern. A red (not maroon) sectional sofa, a king-size bed with a white, padded vinyl headboard, and a yellow chrome dinette set with silver nail heads. Lola remarked, "Where will you find, or how will you afford, bedding for that big bed?"

On weekdays I was alone and my day revolved around planning the evening meal. I tried new recipes and played house with the wedding gifts and hope chest items.

The kitchen was small with no connection to the other two rooms—just a room off a long hall. I snuck around someone else's house—each footstep, each clink of a dish echoed *intruder*. I curled up on my red sofa, closed the door to the hall and spent weeks knitting a sweater for Lee. When it was finished I blocked it and hung it outside to dry. When Lee came that evening he was laughing. When I looked outside I saw Mrs. Palmer sitting in the shade of Lee's sweater. It had doubled in length—a virtual overcoat. Then I made a bedspread for the big bed. Lola was right; I had to piece the top and it took yards and yards of fabric for the taffeta ruffle. Nothing made our rooms a home. I needed a door—and a key.

We put our name on the waiting list for one of the new apartments over the hardware store. I hummed as I spread a turquoise cloth that matched the dainty edge on my Shelly china. Then I folded pink napkins to compliment the roses scattered on the white porcelain. Lola ooh'ed and aah'ed as she sat down, saying, "Barbara, your table is lovely."

I asked, "I think it's pretty, but is my china too formal in the kitchen?"

"No," she said. "The different colored tablecloth and napkins give it a relaxed look."

"Good. I want to use my china and I don't have a dining room."

"One day you will … I'm not sure a dining room is essential anymore."

"Not essential?"

"Not like in my time. We showed our station in life by the table we set. My mother worried that my social status might be compromised without a grand room."

"Really?"

"In fact, she thought I used poor judgment when I married into a family with only a kitchen."

"She did?"

"Yes; but look at me now—the Mayor's wife with a grand formal room."

Dad straightened up, stuck his chest out, and complimented me on my cinnamon rolls.

"But, I don't have a dining room and Lee's hardly the Mayor," I said.

"No, but today you set a distinctive table in your kitchen—you have more choices. Look at this table—one would have to be blind not to recognize your proper upbringing."

Dad buttered another piece of cinnamon roll and said, "If I didn't know better, I would swear your mother baked these rolls. I don't think Lola's mother made cinnamon rolls."

That night I thought about the message to Lola from her mother. Even when she didn't have a dining room she did have a china cabinet. Then I replayed Lola's message to me—I had everything I needed: a home with a door and fine china. But I didn't have a china cabinet or a dining room. I remembered the look on Lola's face the day she slipped the old letter into her pocket; I vowed to someday ask her about that. I dozed off and floated around a magnificent room in a red satin robe tweaking a spectacular table.

The sweater I knit for Lee when we were at the Palmer house was white, fine, and big. I ripped it out and started knitting little sweaters, bonnets, and booties. Lola and Betty came bearing gifts. Lola brought my Bunnykins dishes and Betty had a baby spoon in our silverware pattern. When baby Monica arrived she had a handmade crib, a wardrobe to die for, soft stuffed animals, nursing bottles, gauze Curity diapers, the proverbial silver spoon, and a Royal Doulton place setting.

Formula and diapers, formula and diapers—life in our small apartment revolved around Monica. I moved a quart of milk, a piece of butter, and a pound of ground beef from the old icebox to our new electric refrigerator. The big white box soon filled up with formula and baby food. Lee came home one evening jumping up and down like a Jack-in-the-box and burst out, "You are going to be the first woman in town with a spin-dry washer."

"I need a washing machine, but—" I said

"No buts. It's state-of-the-art," Lee said. "I found it buried in the back of Hodgin's warehouse; I bought it for twenty-five bucks. It only needs a belt."

"It's not new and it doesn't have a wringer?"

"It's a spin dry washer, Barbara. You have a spin-dry washer."

The next evening a huge 45-inch copper tub with legs bracketing an electric motor was in my small kitchen. Inside the tub was a perforated (doughnut shaped) drum to hold the dirty clothes. Lee set about replacing the broken belt and ended up getting a new pulley to fit the only available belt he could find. As he shopped and made the adjustments, he spread the news about his wonderful machine. I tried to appreciate the eyesore in my kitchen.

I had dirty diapers ready as neighbors gathered for a demonstration of our modern marvel. Lee placed the drum on its side to roll through the water—the wash cycle. The neighbors wanted action—they'd come to see it spin. Lee slowly positioned the doughnut flat above the water, and like a conductor about to introduce a crescendo, he leaned forward, waved his hand upward, and then flicked his wrist to engage the spin switch. The copper monstrosity took off and bounced off walls as it careened around the room. The plug finally pulled from its socket as another hole appeared in the wall.

Lee and the neighbors gathered outside in the hall to critique the machine's performance. Alone in my kitchen I wiped my eyes and surveyed the damage. The next morning I bundled up Monica and we went down to the hardware store where we negotiated a deal. Monica's Curity diapers went through a wringer and were hung out to dry.

Monica and I often spent a few days with Lola. We watched their new television, and came home with baby gifts, cookies, jams, and jellies. Lola and Monica developed an innate bond that was magic to behold—they nurtured each other. During one of these visits Dad presented his plan for my future.

Across the country, the first McDonald's franchise opened in Phoenix. At the same time, we sold our first hamburger at the Barb-B-Lee. For the next seventeen years, we worked, lived, raised our children, and played at the Bar-B-Lee.

The business was open from seven in the morning to eleven at night—364 days a year. We were closed on Christmas day. Lee managed the service station, rented snowmobiles, sponsored a hockey team, hauled stock, made deliveries, and chatted with our country customers. I managed the snack bar, prepared menus, checked inventory, kept the books, and decorated. Home and family got squeezed into the few cracks and crevices left by this hectic life style.

I was carrying our second child when we took up residency in the living quarters attached to our new business. When Michael David was born he immediately worked himself into the rhythm of our country store—he was content to watch the players in this unconventional lifestyle. Monica was accustomed to undivided attention and was happiest when she visited with Lola, who was now more than a hundred miles away.

> *Monica remembers: Nannie made me feel I was doing them a favor to visit: I was the princess. We always ate in the dining room. I got to choose the salt and pepper shakers we used. If there was just Nannie, Grandpa, and Me, I picked the yellow ducks. Grandpa always sat at the head of the table, like the King. His water was served from a big glass water pitcher—I guess plastic jugs hadn't been invented yet.*

We expanded our business by adding three more apartments and enlarged the snack bar into a full restaurant. Irene was our cook and every morning she made pies and doughnuts. The restaurant became our prime moneymaker and there was no end to the tables to be set—an art that often verged on drudgery.

My favorite work at the Bar-B-Lee was decorating apartments—creating attractive home spaces. We renovated two units from existing space and rented them to families. I painted one Dresden blue with crisp white woodwork—very traditional. The second was modern with folding doors, and I used a new color combination—flamingo and gray. When I finished a unit I locked the door and, in complete isolation, wandered around thinking about how I would decorate it for Elizabeth Taylor.

Our third child, Perry Thomas Joseph, arrived at the Bar-B-Lee about the same time as our first television set. Perry had an older sister and brother, two busy parents, a handy supply of pie and doughnuts, and a front row seat at the television. He loved music. The Everly Brothers were his favorite, and he and Michael jived to "Jailhouse Rock."

As young couples moved to the suburbs, and built all around us, we built up and added a second story—a home—a place for family—a dining room. I did our new space in a smart black and white pallet with accents of pink and turquoise to compliment my Shelly china. Lola was impressed as her eyes scanned my table.

"Your first dining room … and such a long table," she said.

"Yes, I'll need a larger tablecloth and a couple dozen matching napkins."

"Let me see what I can come up with."

" Great … I wish I had more place settings."

"Shelly is open stock."

"Yes, but they just discontinued my pattern."

"Oh no … we'll have to check for available pieces in the shops."

I had arrived—the head of the house, discussing my dining room and my table settings with Lola, the Mayor's wife.

I had a dining room and entertainment exploded: this didn't necessarily mean more people at my well-set table. Our new living area was large and featured furniture on casters and stacking TV trays. I sometimes presented food on an aluminum foil plate with dividers that resembled a mess tin and served it on a tray with legs. We dined as dignitaries and stars performed for us. We took virtual tours around the world. Family discussions were interrupted as we watched the performance. Entertainment was everywhere. 3-D movies drew TV watchers back to the theater. Teenagers did the Twist. Little girls dressed their Barbie dolls in designer costumes and high heels. Monica mastered the Hula Hoop and entertained Bar-B-Lee's customers with her moves. Disneyland opened in California. And Playboy magazine (in a plain brown wrapper) hit the stands.

One Sunday evening Lola picked up her Shelly plate from my long table and joined Monica and her brothers in front of the Television. They watched *The Wizard of Oz*. Lola marveled, "I can't believe I'm watching this classic with my grandchildren with my dinner in my lap."

As Christmas approached I thought about my first holiday with a dining room—Grandparents, Aunts and Uncles, Nieces and Nephews around my big table. Then I thought about the business being closed—watching the children in their pajamas tear open their packages. A skidoo ride on the snow covered mountain , eating Swanson Turkey TV Dinners as we watched *A Christmas Carol*. No store to contend with, no food to prepare, no table to set.

I sacrificed the table for a day off—I developed guilt scars.

Our new quarters opened onto a sundeck. We had a lit ski slope on our property. There was a skating rink across the road. And the national park around us was open to skidooers in the winter.

The mat inside our front entrance reflected the proliferation of fun and games. What was once a twelve-by-thirty-inch mat was now a four-by six-foot rug—snow boots, skates, ski boots, and skidoo boots piled up each day to drip-dry.

Teenagers drove their own cars and transcontinental jet service changed the way we traveled—the way we lived. I was thirty-two years old when I secretly enlisted a friend to teach me to drive.

I checked the mail every day; then there it was, addressed to me—I had a driver's license. When I showed it to Lee he looked like he'd just got hit by a bus. He whined, "You can't drive a car—no way." I palmed my new license and slid it into my pocket as I walked away, saying, "Just watch me." My driver's license emancipated me: I left to go shopping and have my hair done as I watched the store disappear in my rearview mirror.

Laura's daughter, Judy, was getting married—the little girl Betty and I had babysat when we were going to business college.

> *Betty on Judy's wedding: We traveled first by bus and then by train. We enjoyed a leisurely, childless, lunch. And then we went to a "no appointment necessary" salon where we were bee-hived and lacquered.*

We were all atwitter about our trip home. We had never flown and Dad was treating us to our maiden flight. It was fourteen hours since we had left home. We sat at the airport in our wilted wedding garb and confetti infused, sticky hair, clutching our tickets—afraid we might nod off and miss our flight. We watched, rather matter-of-factly, as the ground disappeared and we climbed above the clouds. After the complimentary coffee and muffin, we dozed until the "prepare for landing" call—the touch down, the speed, the screeching halt. Home in less than an hour.

All my children were in school. Monica was bopping around in rolled up jeans with her hair in a ponytail when I told her we were going to have a new baby.

> *Monica on the new baby: At first I was embarrassed—my old parents were going to have another baby. I was thirteen, a teenager, when the baby arrived. I just prayed it wouldn't be another boy. After the initial shock I was excited: a real baby to play Mom with.*

My pregnancy afforded me the privilege of house time. I set the table for the whole family, but the family didn't function on the same schedule. Home was a mountain resort where everyone worked. Monica had a part-time job in the restaurant and Michael worked in the service station. Home was not a sanctuary where the family sat down together.

> *Monica on working in the store: I hated the store. We couldn't be a normal family. Normal didn't have to be <u>Leave it to Beaver</u> or <u>Father Knows Best</u>, just off on weekends and time spent together. Do you believe we didn't have a dishwasher in that restaurant?*

Lisa Lou was born into a family of big people. For the first five years of her life she claimed everyone's love and demanded everyone's attention as family members came and went—like the changing of the guard.

Lee attended his sister's funeral in Florida and returned home to a massive ice storm. It was decided: we put the 'Bar-B-Lee' up for sale—we moved south. Before we moved, Monica surprised me. She spent her paycheck and bought all the pieces of Shelly she could find. I was ecstatic. Like my ancestors before me, I moved fine china across the country to set my table in a more traditional home.

I set tables
In the kitchen,
In a restaurant,
In my first dining room,
In front of the television.

Chapter 8 - Monica Sets Her Table

At the White House:

In 1966 Lady Bird Johnson ordered the first full set of china since the Truman china in 1951. First Lady Patricia Nixon presented it to the public. First Lady Betty Ford chose it for her large formal dinners.

At the Same Time:

Monica sets her first table with silver banded, white porcelain on a navy cloth.

Now I knew how Lola had felt when she moved from the farm to the Mayor's house. I had a house without a business attached. I had a home—a refuge, a place to entertain, new horizons. The house was a typical three-bedroom home with new extensions. It was open with outdoor spaces—a lanai, a swimming pool, a dock. Private spots to play. And play we did. The children jumped in and out of the pool. We had boats at the dock ready to board. Sets of golf clubs hung in the garage and were ready for the links.

Betty and Lola, my sources of support and influence, were thousands of miles away. I stood alone—a pioneer, challenged and vulnerable. I emptied my valise of stored-up passions. I gathered all my family around the table every day. I had time with Lisa. I watched Monica become a woman.

Everyone had to work to support this wonderful new life style. Lee and Michael found work in their fields of experience. Neither Monica nor I wanted anything to do with a restaurant. Monica did not focus on a career.

> *Monica's thought: I hoped to work 9 to 5 Monday through Friday and have the weekends off. I was eighteen. I wanted friends, a social life, and freedom to do nothing or anything.*

Lee brought co-workers home for dinner—prospective suitors for Monica. The first was a good-looking doctor's son who liked the bar scene and sold table settings on the side. Monica loved the dishes. The second man was seven years older than Monica. He was looking for a wife. Monica had a magnificent set of silver banded, white porcelain and a proposal. We had a wedding to plan.

> *Monica's thoughts: Will was cute and liked to party—this was fun for a while. Len wanted marriage and a family. I think that is what I wanted— to be needed.*

Monica was in the spotlight. She primped as she modeled white lace gowns. She postured as she draped yards and yards of purple satin for her attendants' gowns. She watched as I mixed, baked, and iced a three-tier wedding cake. She chose wedding bells for the topper. One hundred and fifty invitations were addressed. We ordered flowers and out-of-town guests responded. The groom faded into the shadows as Monica's fairytale developed—according to Great-Aunt Margaret's protocol.

We set the head table with Shelly china on a white linen cloth. Dozens of pink roses upstaged the china. Guest tables were overlaid with purple tulle and centered with sweet peas. Monica embraced each detail, each preparation—it was her inauguration.

We were ready to leave for the church. Lisa, in her purple, satin flower girl's dress, tugged on Monica's lace skirt, reached for her hand and said, "This is supposed to be the happiest day of your life." Monica gave a condescending smile and straightened Lisa's bangs. I shivered.

I tried to put the scene in perspective. I was a mother-in-law invited for dessert—fondue. Monica's table was dramatic. I exclaimed, "Monica, your navy cloth and napkins are a perfect pallet for your china."

Monica smiled, "Yes, but I'm not sure about the serving dishes; the fondue pot with the fruit and cake bowls—should they match?"

"No, the glass and silver compliment each other and add interest."

"But ... a cooking pot on my dining room table?"

"It's not a pot. It's never been on the stove."

"I suppose ... It's the first time I've served fondue."

"It's the first time we've had fondue ... a real treat."

Lee and Len made jokes about the small servings and having to cook. Lisa filled a bowl with fruit and cake cubes and sat on the floor. An unconventional table, but the table was set. The family was gathered, and there was laughter. All was as it should be—perhaps.

Monica's view: Nannie and Mum made family gatherings seem easy. Entertaining Mum was hard. Fondue was not a workingman's idea of food; they had no class.

Monica's marriage set off a chain reaction, and our family portrait changed. Lisa started school, Michael married Linda, Perry joined the Navy, and Monica gave birth. I was a grandmother.

Lisa was the only child at home. I was secretly elated about the prospect of a career. Butterflies fluttered around my head, just waiting to light: a paycheck, a briefcase, a title, and my own car. Our newly incorporated city offered positions with excellent benefits. I studied each new listing. I soon discovered the positions I qualified for did not excite me. I was about to look at other venues when a new position reached out and grabbed me. Police Radio Dispatcher: coordinating police, fire, and ambulance. The more I thought about it, the more excited I got.

I told Monica that I was considering applying for a job in the police department, and she told me she wanted to apply for a position with an accounting firm on the beach. We fed off each other's enthusiasm. She put her firstborn in day care: my lastborn, Lisa, was in school.

The Major, who interviewed me, promised training, advances, a badge, a title, and my choice of shift. I left with a position. I drove home with my head full of plans. The responsibility of my position was immediately obvious. I asked questions, read, and developed new techniques. I was the first grandmother to graduate from basic recruit school at the police academy. On my one year anniversary the Pilot Club honored me as "Outstanding Woman in Law Enforcement."

Monica found her niche, too. She loved working with figures and received recognition and a promotion. But, she had a long commute and was expected to take full responsibility for the baby and household—there was stress at home. They filed for divorce.

Monica adjusts: When we divorced, I got to be ME. I enjoyed my work as an accountant. I felt important and appreciated. I was good at what I did. I knew no one was indispensable, but I felt that way.

My children were in new relationships—pioneers. I was experiencing withdrawal symptoms. I needed to spend time with Lola. As my plane landed, I anticipated coming home—being mothered, everything being okay. I found Lola old and feeble. My father was lying on the couch chewing his fingernail. They needed help; they talked about assisted living.

I picked up Kentucky Fried Chicken for dinner. As I set the dining room table and found the serving dishes for the chicken, I thought about Lola the day she slipped the old letter in her pocket. I needed to know why that letter drove her.

Dad finally shuffled off to bed and I made Lola and me a cup of tea. We sat at the dining room table dunking sugar cookies. I told Lola, "I am uneasy … my children are leaving home and I have a new career. Nothing is familiar and I don't have a map." Lola warmed her gnarled hands on her teacup and finally spoke. "If we are lucky we move through many different phases of our existence. We need to grab each new offer and live it to the fullest."

"You have done that," I said.

"Yes, I ran the house at Dell Farm. Then I presided as the Mayor's Wife, and now I will enjoy assisted living."

"I hope I can do as much."

"You will do more. You have more choices—more time."

"Tell me about the old letter."

"What old letter?"

"The one you slipped into your pocket in this room the day they delivered this furniture."

"You saw that?"

"Yes. Can you tell me about it?"

Lola shifted her position and poured another cup of tea. "My mother wrote it to me when I married your dad. She had such a fine dining room—contemporary in her day, finished in the new tiger stripe grain. From a little girl, I cut primroses and arranged them for the centerpiece."

"Was that a primrose in the old letter?"

"Yes, her way of reminding me of my upbringing. She wanted me to have a dining room. She thought it was necessary to show one's positions in life."

"What did you think?"

Lola fiddled with her hair and squared her shoulders. "It is all in the way one carries oneself—the way they set their table, the presentation. I saw that demonstrated when I was in college, and again tonight when you put dinner on this table. It is always about the presentation. The location is secondary. Now, I always wanted a grand room like my mother's. And when I stacked the Barratts and Balmoral in the new china cabinet, it made me happy. I had exceeded my mother's wishes for me. That night, when you were all in bed, I sat in front of the fireplace, drank tea from one of the new cups, and watched the letter burn. I kept the rose."

Six months after my visit, Dad died. Lola squared her shoulders and presented herself to assisted living.

Lisa was doing well in school; she participated in science projects and public speaking. Monica had found her career path and juggled it with motherhood and dating. I joined a National Public Safety Communication organization and become the first female president for the Florida Chapter. I traveled as a technical adviser and consultant. I presented a bill to the Florida Legislature for compulsory State Certification for Telecommunicators.

Monica met Randy. They married on the lanai beside the pool. Michael's wife, Linda, a Justice of the Peace, officiated. Monica and her Matron-of-Honor wore street length summer print dresses. The cake was from the local bakery and Monica chose a bride and groom for the topper. There were dozens of yellow roses. Many floated on the pool: a pretty wedding that would have received Great-Aunt Margaret's stamp of approval for a second wedding.

I was recognized throughout the State as an authority on public safety communications. At home my position gave fodder for sexist's jokes. I enjoyed my home and I set my table with the same passion with which I advanced my career, but there were fewer places to set. Lee and I did not have a common goal for the rest of our life.

Monica went with me to file for divorce. I didn't want to burden her with the separation, but she insisted. It was her first try at mothering me. She took my arm—I cried.

We sold our traditional home. I bought a condominium and Lisa and I moved in. We both had our first date. Lisa got her driver's license. I bought her first car for her—then, one at a time, four new fenders. Monica and I both bought one of the new microwave ovens.

Monica on a career with a microwave: Cooking from scratch was impossible if you wanted to eat before nine. The microwave was a real help. Take a can, add something to it, doctor it up, nuke it.

Lisa had a part-time job as a hostess at a local restaurant. She joined the forensic team at college and traveled throughout the state competing: she had an aptitude for impromptu public speaking. Lisa was passionate about each new interest. She had no ceiling—no limit to her expectations. We usually sat down at the table for our evening meal. There was conflict. We did not like each other's male friends.

One evening, Asa, a new friend of mine, was having dinner with us. Lisa and I were lamenting about having eaten too much desert. Asa used his southern drawl: "You girls don't have to worry;

everything you eat just turns to pretty." Lisa rolled her eyes, asked to be excused, and under her breath said, "I feel a little nauseous."

> *Lisa on life at the condo: I remember when you got that microwave. Frozen dinners became the norm because we were both so busy. I liked my bedroom because you let me decorate it like a living room.*

Monica gave birth to her second child and was nesting nicely with her new family and successful career when Lisa dropped her bombshell: she was going to marry. She was seventeen, career bound, and marrying a man who had no ambition and was old enough to be her father. He was good looking.

As Lisa planned her wedding, I grounded myself with Lola's words: "It's all in the presentation; the location is secondary." The wedding was at her father's home. They had a hot tub with a waterfall—a suitable backdrop for the nuptials. I directed my efforts to the presentation—Lisa's white gown, a three-tier cake, a hand-crocheted tablecloth, and a wide-brimmed floppy hat for me.

A family transitioned: everyone playing a new part—and no choreographer. Only Linda knew her lines as she officiated at her second family wedding. Lisa said, "I do." I did not present myself well. I felt like the family spinster who had dropped in for free cake and champagne. There were questions about my hat. I questioned Lola's theory that location was secondary. Two months later Lisa drew up and filed her divorce papers. She stayed with Monica until she figured out her next move.

> *Lisa chimes in: I don't think that it was only two months, but it was quick. Like you, Mother, I sought independence from a young age and took the first path that I thought would lead to it. In retrospect, I should have just moved out on my own. But things turned out OK!*

The Mayor held his prayer book, the photographer loaded his camera, and my friend Bea clutched her purse: they all wiggled into the back of the plane. Asa, in a crisp white shirt and pinstripe suit, sat in the pilot's seat. I buckled into the co-pilot's seat wearing a long maroon moiré skirt and a white lace blouse. We taxied and took off. The camera snapped. We banked and circled. The mayor read his lines. We said, "I do."

Great-aunt Margaret would have questioned this wedding flight—she would have approved of the reception that followed.

Marriages fail.

Careers soar.

New tables are set.

Chapter 9 - A New Role: A New Table

At the White House:

Rosalynn Carter, a small-town girl from Georgia, inspired the nation with her independence and commanded the world's attention when she traveled the globe as a special presidential envoy. She stood close to the center of power in American government and understood the hopes and dreams of the American people. First Lady Rosalynn Carter found the china in the White House fascinating. Upstairs they used the Woodrow Wilson china. Downstairs they used the Truman china with the wide green band and the Johnson china, trimmed with wild flowers. So even for large formal dinners, there was plenty of china.

At the Same Time:

I use white pottery in my kitchen, Shelly rosebud in the dining room, and pink plastic, glass, and tin on the lanai. For large functions I set all three tables and mixed pottery, porcelain, and synthetics.

W e coasted through white clouds, at times blinded by their drift; then through banks of snowy fluff to maneuver and slalom around. For a moment I was the naive kid holding on to Gordie Alexander as he piloted his red sloop sleighs down the hill behind the schoolhouse. The drone of the Cessna 310 brought me into the now. The pilot was old and softer, but the feeling of adventure and freedom was the same. I was entering a new phase of my existence—I grabbed on and flew.

    We co-habited as individuals. Asa spent his mornings keeping books. I suggested a computer. He put his ledger on the shelf and mastered spreadsheets—everything was counted. I loved the house and started decorating—made it mine. I erased a sea of avocado green. Asa liked the new look and suggested I consider interior decorating and color consulting: Style Brokers International and Personal Statement were incorporated and I took on a couple of clients. Asa enrolled in a French cooking class and I attended ground school for my pilot's license. We flew. I sat in the right seat and co-piloted on weekend flights to Vail, Chicago, and the Bahamas. We asked about local cuisine and interesting restaurants. We soaked up the ambience of the expanse, quietly in sync, sitting at a table.

We dined. At home Asa cooked, I cooked, or we fended for ourselves. We sat at the kitchen table, the patio table, or the dining room table, depending on the whim, the event, or the weather. No matter the table, no matter the table settings, there were soft white cloth napkins to wipe and dab. For family visits, holidays, and our annual birthday party, we set all three tables (Once a year we had a birthday party for our five grandsons—on no one's birthday.). Place settings for these grand events were assembled from twelve place settings of white earthenware, eight place settings of Shelly Rosebud, and a hodge-podge of glass, plastic, and tin. Tables that celebrated diversity were anchored with pink linen, lace, or denim cloths: tin cups, crystal goblets, heavy pottery, and fine porcelain were layered and coupled. Tradition and exotics mingled amicably.

We flew and had dining extravaganzas. Betty, Ronnie, and four of their friends were vacationing at a resort just south of us. We landed the King Air at their small airport, picked them up, and flew them to Miami for dinner. The take-off for our return flight was spectacular—from a grid of pink streetlights into a star-spangled night sky. At an annual birthday party for our five grandsons, Asa flew them over each of their homes. Back on earth they sat down to my masterpiece: a sandwich village, complete with peanut butter roads and match boxcars and trucks.

It was time for Asa to meet Lola. She was thriving in her new assisted living digs. I wondered about her acceptance of my new husband. She and the other residents might be shocked by my brazen lifestyle—divorced and married to a southerner. We stayed with Betty and Ronnie and decided to go white-water rafting while in the area.

Before he met Lola I drove Asa by the Dell Farm and the mayor's house. As I looked through his eyes, my roots deteriorated—my pedigree tarnished. Lola was waiting in the reception room, dressed in a soft tailored pantsuit—contemporary garb. She stood and presented herself. Her wrinkles added depth to the lady she was. Asa met the First Lady of Dell Farm, the Mayor's Wife, and the Grande Matron of Assisted Living.

Lunch with Lola was a step into a past generation. Everyone wore hose with the appropriate afternoon dress. The men wore a tie and the women carried a bag—hankie and pills handy. Everyone was wrinkled and polite. The individual tables were set with china and silverware on a tablecloth with matching soft napkins. Lola introduced Asa as "Barbara's new husband." Asa turned on his charm and asked the men about the river we were going to raft the next day. He told the women how pretty they looked in whatever they are wearing. "The Lodge" buzzed for weeks with comments about Barbara and her new husband.

We enjoyed our visit with Betty and Ronnie and white-water rafting was exhilarating, but our time with Lola was the highlight.

Lola had a wonderful Sunday as she attended services in the newly decorated church, down the street from the mayor's house. After service she and Laura had lunch with the congregation in the basement meeting rooms. It was a social event to rededicate the refurbished church, and Lola Ooh'ed and Aah'ed. Sitting in her easy chair, back at the Lodge, reflecting on her wonderful day, she entered the next phase of her existence. The church was ready to celebrate her passing.

Computers changed the way we lived. The world was at our fingertips; time was our only barrier. With a computer in-house, Asa signed a contract to manage a condominium complex. More time with numbers excited him. I enrolled in an accelerated program for a Bachelor's Degree in Professional Studies, and after that for a Master's Degree in Business. The computer hummed eight to ten hours each day. Computers were the driving force at work too. 9-1-1 and computer-aided dispatch changed emergency communications. I hired more operators and developed new training programs. The Internet was launched. Perry (the little boy who loved song and grew up with the television) perused Silicone Valley and wrote software for computerized music.

With more and more fast-food restaurants and computers processing more and more information faster and faster, people were eating at a computer desk or in their car—from a piece of paper. We set the table.

Asa was at the computer when the Space Shuttle Enterprise blasted off for its maiden voyage—he knew he would never fly in space. He looked at our Shelly inventory on the screen and appreciated its value. He thought about retiring his pilot's license and buying a boat.

I stepped onto the escalator, put my two shopping bags down, and flexed my tired shoulders. I looked out over the Christmas decorations and there it was—a red satin robe. With one hand on the big, gift-wrapped box, I maneuvered through holiday traffic. I was filled with anticipation. I wrapped myself in my red gown and presented myself to Asa. I set the table and served Christmas breakfast in it. I tied a matching red bow on the cell phone I had bought for Asa and served it to him on a silver tray. He loved the presentation and wallowed in being one of the first to have a cell phone.

On Christmas evening we sat on the dock watching the sunset behind our new boat. I was feeling very festive in my red housecoat. I exposed one leg and asked Asa if he was ready for bed. He answered, "Not yet. I have a phone call to make." He pulled his cell phone from his robe pocket and called Ronnie. He wished him a Merry Christmas and mentioned that he was calling on his new cell phone and sitting on the dock beside his new boat. He added that I was looking mighty sexy in my red robe.

We drank coffee, read the morning paper, and watched our new boat bob on the incoming tide. I took inventory of the scene and said, "Now that we are both retired, let's plan a boat trip."

Asa put the paper down, cleared his throat, and gave me his full attention. "Where would you like to go?" he asked.

"On a real adventure—a voyage."

"We could go to the Keys."

"No! No! Like up the Intracoastal; maybe into Canada a bit."

"My God! You dream big! We can plan, buy charts ... maybe in a year or two."

"We're both in good shape now. The boat is in good shape. That could all change in a year or two."

"But this is a huge undertaking. We need to plan—be prepared."

"I agree. We can buy charts, guidebooks, and maybe one of those new GPS gadgets."

Talk of the GPS did it. We spent a couple of afternoons in the boat store and days plotting courses and testing the GPS in local waters. We outfitted the boat with an air conditioner, a television, a microwave, and place settings for two. We stowed provisions: tools, canned goods, and clothes. As I wiggled my make-up kit into an overhead compartment, with the charts and the GPS, I thought about my ancestor stowing the crystal knife rests in the bag of flour in the bow of her canoe. Like her, I could be called on to make a sacrifice—my lipstick and mascara for the GPS and the charts. On the first day of May we pushed off from our dock—onto our voyage north.

We were still in Florida waters when we had to batten down the hatches, evacuate the boat, and take shelter from high winds and heavy rain. We were under a tornado watch. Back on the water we had our first mechanical problem and holed up in a second-rate motel, waiting for a part to be shipped from the other coast. Neither of us mentioned returning home or discontinuing our journey. Underway again we put home farther and farther behind us. Each night we read the guidebooks and plotted our course.

We dined in a five-star restaurant, set in a refurbished facility that outfitted Benedict Arnold's fleet. We ate the catch of the day at marina restaurants. I served creamed salmon over rice in the galley and nachos on the aft deck—always at a table on a plate.

We traveled on flat water, on choppy water, and through swells. We navigated through fog, rain, and blinding sun—always on a GPS-charted course. Every night we put in at a marina, plugged in the air conditioning, and had "happy hour" on the aft deck.

On July 3rd at Sandy Hook Marina, we plotted our course through New York Harbor. We pushed off at the crack of dawn, excited and nervous, anticipating major traffic in the harbor; we were a miniature intruder navigating amongst the giants. There was radio traffic from a Russian freighter, but only the Staten Island Ferry was under way as we followed our course to the Lady. My first look at the Statue was through the mist. The hair stood up on my arms as I snapped pictures and set the aft table. It was the 4th of July and our little boat idled alone at the foot of the Statue of Liberty. We sat down to a breakfast of baked beans and biscuits served in red Fiesta bowls on a navy terry cloth. We raised champagne glasses and toasted our being.

Up the Hudson, through the Erie Canal, and across the tip of Lake Ontario into Canada— we had arrived at our destination. The Rideau River, the Ottawa River, the St. Lawrence Seaway, and Lake Champlain brought us back onto The Hudson River and homeward. An old couple in their little boat, hobnobbing with explorers, set their table in the wake of history.

Back at home we cocooned as John Travolta discoed and Lisa built her professional career and became another independent woman of the family.

> We flew.
> We sailed.
> We dined.

Chapter 10 - Full Circle: A China Cabinet in My Kitchen

At the White House:

Like other First Ladies before her, Nancy Reagan planned for a new service that would accommodate the scale of anticipated entertaining and reflect her personal interest in setting a table with formal elegance. The service attracted much public attention because of its color and expense. Margaret Truman Daniel came to the First Lady's defense: "When the President and First Lady give a state dinner, the china should match."

At the Same Time:

Lisa's place settings attracted attention—hanging on her wall. Each move, each new career, warrants a table and place setting—they were symbols. Lisa forged her way into corporate offices across the nation. Computers, the Internet, headhunters, and company-paid relocations fueled her spirit of adventure.

After many days at sea it was good to be home. I toyed with the morning paper and watched a boat meander through the river. I thought about our vacation on one of those huge cruise ships—was it time and money well spent? I saw Hawaii and I spent time with Betty. The ship's interior was luxurious. There were people from all over the world—unidentifiable, universal. In tee shirts, jeans, shorts, and canvas shoes, they walked on thick carpet and marble stairs, rubbed against brass railings, and leaned on the grand piano. The dining experience made it meaningful. Mimicking Great-Aunt Margaret's morning, afternoon, and social dress, the passengers shed their "comfy sloppy" for "classy casual" and formal. Guests and table settings sparkled—diamonds, crystal, brocade, silver, satin, fresh flowers, and candlelight in magnificent competition. Three times each day, I dined with interesting people, fittingly attired, at a proper table—a concept Lola had introduced me to at Dell Farm.

A mirage of boats, ships, crystal, silverware, and china went round and round in my head. From the crystal trivets my ancestors had stowed in the bow of their canoe to the wine glasses Asa and I had shelved on-board our cabin cruiser, to traversing the Pacific on a luxury liner, the measure of the lifestyle was reflected in table settings. A legacy I needed to pass on.

My new sideboard held props that reflected the progression of our family lifestyle. My Shelly china service was primary. Some pieces had been a gift from my first wedding. Some Monica had bought with her first paycheck. And others I had ordered from Replacements Unlimited. There was a bevy of cut-glass plates I used when the ladies gathered for bridge—candy dishes, butter dishes, cake plates, and gravy boats—some Aunt Margaret's, some Lola's, some gifts from my children. The burgundy cordial glass with "Lola" etched on its flange held toothpicks. A crystal martini pitcher with a broken stirrer inside was used as a vase for fresh cut roses. A brown and white English china platter was the one remaining piece from my mother and father's wedding china. A tarnished silver bowl with "Outstanding Woman in Law Enforcement" engraved on its side. Coffee spoons with a gold nugget on each handle that Mother and Dad had bought in the Yukon Territories the day Monica was born. Three candles in hand-painted glass trivets—Lisa's handiwork. Two cups, one saucer, and a pitcher—remnants of Great-Aunt Margaret's cocoa set. And two letters painstakingly word-processed—one for Monica and one for Lisa.

I wondered if I had produced suitable venues to ensure the legacy of my china cabinet. My Shelly Rosebud was on the endangered species list, and I could not bear to have it warehoused. Today fine china is losing its habitat: punctual diners in their best attire. Fine table linens, silver, crystal, and dining rooms are all falling victim to a casual lifestyle.

As I sat with a planning list in hand, I focused my eyes upward to some imagined china god and lamented. I wanted my china to showcase Friday night's dinner. I could provide the traditional in-house habitat, but my guests would not cohabit comfortably—there would be jeans and at least one baseball cap. I sighed and whispered, "Great-Aunt Margaret would know what to do."

But maybe not. Great-Auntie had dealt with immigrants with a similar heritage. Today she would have encountered a more diverse group.

"Diversity," I cried to my dish deity. "Diversity is the problem."

In a soft echo came the reply: "Could it be the solution?"

Could my Shelly maintain its influence on those around my table if it mingled with exotics? Great-Aunt Margaret would know. She once plunked a chamber pot in the center of the table and filled it with lilacs to match those on the china. I had to neutralize and assimilate the exotics, feature my fine china, and create a casual ambiance.

To neutralize guests' jeans, I made a denim tablecloth. I layered it over pink linen or under white lace. My granddaughter had jeans with lace pockets. I wrote on my list: pink, plastic place settings, tin cups, and galvanized chargers.

The plastic tumblers, tin cups, and a crystal wine glass here and there drowned out the beer cans and paper cups. Tardy guests caused less of a disruption in the casual setting. I wondered what to do about the baseball caps.

Come Friday I was ready. As I set the table I thought about the proliferation of things at my disposal: inexpensive, frivolous nonessentials; use-a-while-and-replace items, wild things that needed to be corralled and anchored by tradition. So I layered denim and lace, stacked china, plastic, and tin, and grouped crystal stemware, tin cups, and plastic tumblers. I created a table where diversity was celebrated and tradition honored.

My guests arrived. As my grandson's eyes darted from china to plastic to tin, he slid one hand up the back of his neck and deftly folded his ball cap into his open palm. The cap disappeared.

Great-Aunt Margaret smiled.

Afterword

We lost our mother, Barbara McCranie, in April 2006. Asa died a year before her in 2005. During her final year, our mother focused on two activities: buying and remodeling a condominium and working on her memoir (this book). Her two-bedroom condo went from an ugly duckling to a wonderful and classy personification of Mother's style and upbringing. At the time she died from a stroke, the condo was perfect and her memoir nearly done.

While I did not inherit my mother's sense of style regarding place settings, I am a writer and was asked by the family to prepare Mother's book for publication. And so this is what I have done. I learned a few things about my mother and myself in the process. Mostly, I came to deeply appreciate my mother's sense of independence and adventure—traits she and I shared.

Mom's prized Shelly china found new appreciation at Monica's home.

I set my table with bright Fiestaware of many colors. Mother embraced and encouraged my love of bright colors, even though her preferred color palette was much more subdued and refined. For three years and up until she died, she periodically shipped me one Fiestaware place setting in the latest color. My husband and I have more Fiestaware than we will ever know what to do with, but we are no longer up-to-date with the newest colors.

Mother's plan was to ask former First Lady Rosalynn Carter to write the Foreword, and to donate all proceeds from her book to Habitat for Humanity. She wanted her tribute to the well-set table to help set tables for other families. To honor her original intent, we will be donating all the proceeds from this book to Habitat for Humanity.

On the following pages are two short pieces: one written by Mother and a poem I wrote after her death. On behalf of my family and me, we hope you have enjoyed reading our mother's final labor of love, *Place Settings in Time*.

Lisa Haneberg
Daughter of Barbara McCranie

Evidence of a Good Life

By Barbara McCranie

I feel good about the weirdest things. This week I'm wallowing in the recognition that our worn table napkins validate a fine lifestyle. Not just great dining, but a higher level of living.

It started when my husband suggested new napkins. The dozen white cotton dinner napkins are still good and proof of thousands of dinners for two. The same old couple dabbing and wiping until their napkins are threadbare. You can't replace that.

Worn table napkins are symbolic of the soft touch of wrinkled hands, worn elbow patches on a favorite sweater, a book with dog-eared pages, a fireplace stained by smoke—a testimony of a meaningful life.

New napkins would offer a promise; old ones are evidence.

On a list of wishes for my children: worn napkins.

Mom's Coleslaw
By Lisa Haneberg

Never a very good cook -
colorless shoe leather roasts,
canned creamed corn,
ketchup saved the day.
Mom had three masterpieces -
sweet dark mushy baked beans,
tart apple pie stacked high,
fresh-tasting coleslaw.

Slice then cube green cabbage,
dice snappy red apples,
chop ribbons of sweet onion,
together with a pinch of salt.
Mix mayonnaise with a splash
of milk to dressing consistency
add a tablespoon or two of sugar
coat cabbage, apples, and onions.

Mom used to make coleslaw
whenever the family gathered.
She chose a cobalt crystal bowl
to show off the slaw's milky
elegance and simple taste.
Mom set a fine dinner table,
fussing over the feast's
plates and platters.

As we cleaned out Mom's condo,
my sister handed me the blue bowl.
My turn to make Mom's Coleslaw.
I think she'd find it strange that cabbage,
mayo, milk, sugar, and apples
would fuel memories,
a flood of salt,
and a tender sense of her near.